The Work of the Church Treasurer

Thomas E. McLeod

A manual of practical instruction for the newly elected church treasurer or financial secretary. Especially helpful for the smaller church, this guide provides specific instructions based on sound business practices for overall financial planning, developing a practical financial system, and maintaining all necessary records.

Judson Press® Valley Forge

The Work of the Church Treasurer—Revised Edition

Copyright © 1981, 1992
Judson Press, Valley Forge, PA 19482-0851

Library of Congress Cataloging-in-Publication Data

McLeod, Thomas E.
    The work of the church treasurer / Thomas E. McLeod. — Rev. ed.
       p.   cm.
    ISBN 0-8170-1189-7 :
    1. Church finance—Accounting. I. Title.
    BV773.M3 1992   92-23564
    254.8—dc20   CIP

05 04 03 02 01 00 99 98
11 10 9 8 7 6 5 4 3

Contents

List of Exhibits   3

Preface   5

Chapter **1   Basic Guidelines**   7

Chapter **2   The Budget**   11

Chapter **3   Cash Receipts**   17

Chapter **4   Cash Disbursements**   23

Chapter **5   Accounting Rules and Procedures**   27

Chapter **6   The Accounting Process Illustrated**   33

Chapter **7   Reporting**   55

Chapter **8   Computer Applications**   63

Appendix   **Software Vendors**   67

Glossary of Terms   69

List of Exhibits

2–1	Sample Church Budget Worksheet	13
2–2	Budget Request Form	14
2–3	Pledge Card	16
3–1	Offering Envelope	18
3–2	Offering Envelope as Marked	18
3–3	Deposit Slip	19
3–4	Report of Deposit	20
3–5	Member Contribution Record	21
4–1	Chart of Budget Accounts	24
4–2	Sample Church Disbursement Requisition	25
4–3	Blank Check and Stub	26
4–4	Voucher Check	26
6–1	Cash Receipts and Disbursements Journal	34
6–2	Ledger Accounts, Sample Church	42
6–3	Sample Church Trial Balance	51
7–1	Sample Church Statement of Cash Receipts and Disbursements	57
7–2	Sample Church Summary of Operating Fund Receipts and Disbursements and Fund Balances	59
7–3	Statement of Cash Receipts, Disbursements, and Fund Balances (for Checking and Savings)	61

Preface

There are two purposes of *The Work of the Church Treasurer:* (1) to explain how to develop sound business practices and procedures in the church environment; (2) to show how to apply them in step-by-step fashion to an entire bookkeeping cycle beginning with development of a budget, recording transactions, and reporting actual and budgeted amounts.

Churches of all sizes need to establish policies that will ensure control and accuracy. Thus, the first purpose addresses the needs of larger churches that have an established accounting system. Smaller churches that may not have an established system would be concerned with both purposes.

In the past decade the computer has assumed an expanded role in processing essential data in business, government, and not-for-profit organizations. This new technology not only makes processing faster and easier, but also makes it possible to generate new and better information. Most readers who are considering using a computer for the first time will probably want to look at the capability of the smaller personal computers rather than the larger mainframe computers. To help in your search, the final chapter briefly explores computer features and capabilities and procedures for setting up a system. After you have studied most of the basic accounting ideas and business practices presented herein, you should be prepared for either method of record keeping.

This book, in its original edition, has proven to be helpful to churches in an age that demands accountability. Therefore, aside from the addition of computer information and the updating of social security tax requirements, few changes have been made. The importance of this book's role in helping churches handle funds responsibly is underscored by news reports of mishandling of funds. These reports remind us of the need for better control over funds entrusted to individuals, churches, businesses, and governmental agencies. This basic need for controls has in fact become more important in an age when the computer can be used in schemes to misappropriate funds.

Newly organized churches may find it somewhat easier than older, established churches to adopt recommended control procedures. In any case, financial custodians want to uphold the high level of trust placed in them. My intent in writing this book is to make it possible for your church to attain this goal. These ideas and suggestions, coupled with a treasurer's willingness to explain to church members how the financial controls actually work, should result in a smoothly functioning financial system.

Chapter 1
Basic Guidelines

The church that attains worthwhile goals must engage in planning, implementing plans, and following up to measure accomplishment. In each of these steps financial matters are involved that must be recognized. Church programs cost both time and money. An essential ingredient of success is proper use and control of these resources. While the financial side of the church is not an end in itself, good financial planning and control can help the church achieve its objectives of providing growth opportunities for its members and service to the community at large. Regardless of its size, a church can utilize sound business practices and procedures as a means of helping it achieve its primary goal and objectives.

While a large church has problems and needs that are somewhat different from a smaller church's, the size of church organization or the number of members has little to do with the need for keeping adequate records. This book gives instructions that can be applied in all churches, but its major objective is to provide help for financial secretaries, treasurers, bookkeepers, and perhaps accountants, especially in smaller churches that do not employ full-time bookkeepers or accountants. It will be useful as a guide. Each of the chapters that follows gives specific instructions about financial matters from preparing the budget to the actual keeping of records of receipts and disbursements and preparing the reports. However, before going into specific procedures, this chapter discusses overall financial planning by describing policies the church should adopt to achieve better control over the entire financial spectrum. Most of the material in this chapter will be of interest to the pastor and church staff as well as to lay persons in leadership capacities. Selected topics in the remaining chapters should also be read as determined by the interest of the person and his or her organizational function.

Assuming that your church is interested in adopting practices and procedures to help it get the most out of its financial resources, how should it begin? What steps are necessary? Who should be responsible? While a number of suggestions are offered in the discussion that follows, any plan that is developed should be consistent with a church's constitution and bylaws, which define the organizational structure and designate responsibility. Here are some of the major items that should be considered for possible inclusion in such documents. The items are presented under two major headings: (1) the organizational plan and (2) essential business functions. No attempt is made in the discussion to prescribe the specific wording or content of the documents your church should adopt. Rather, each church should adopt the wording that would best suit its needs. The reader should also note that some of the discussion material deals with specific procedures that would be inappropriate for church bylaws. These procedures need to be adopted by the church perhaps as a separate document because they may be subject to occasional revision.

Plan of Organization

Even the smallest church needs a plan of organization that assigns responsibility. To achieve control over financial matters as well as the actual operations, planning must begin at the top of the organization. In a church the members collectively delegate authority and responsibility to lay leaders, the pastor, and other employees. While not absolutely essential, a constitution and bylaws are desirable to specify an organizational structure. Persons working to accomplish their assigned duties need to have identified for them specific responsibilities for handling financial affairs. Any important policies should be adopted by the members of the church. The membership has not fulfilled its duty until it adopts broad guidelines that specify checks and balances to protect the staff and others who handle financial transactions. The guidelines should be such that no single employee or member could either accidentally or intentionally misappropriate funds or even make a significant error that would go undetected for any length of time. To accomplish this goal, several functions or positions are necessary. At the minimum these should include the treasurer, finance committee, trustees, and personnel committee as well as the pastor and staff. A brief description of each of these is presented next.

Treasurer

Designate the treasurer as the person responsible to be custodian of the church's funds and other liquid assets and to keep the records. But to achieve a satisfactory level of control, this person must not be the sole individual concerned with the receiving and spending of cash. In many churches the treasurer is the most experienced person in financial matters and is given almost complete charge over cash received and disbursed, a policy that is not desirable from a control standpoint. The treasurer should be responsible for writing all checks and for rendering periodic reports to the membership. If the church employs either a full-time or part-time financial secretary, most of the actual check-writing and record-keeping functions will be performed by that person. Two signatures should be required on all checks, one of which may be that of the treasurer.

Finance Committee

This committee should consist of at least three members, with one who will serve as chairperson. Its primary function is to coordinate the preparation and implementation of the annual budget or forecast. The committee must obtain from the pastor, staff, and organizational heads their estimates of financial needs for the coming year. If the church wishes to secure budget pledges from its members, this will be done by the committee after the budget is adopted. Finally, the committee is responsible for making the budget work. If needed, the chairperson should work directly with the treasurer in seeing that expenditures are charged to the appropriate budget categories and accounts.

Trustees

Trustees are responsible for maintenance of buildings and grounds as well as of furniture and equipment. Three or more persons should be selected for this important role who have expertise in the purchase and upkeep of buildings and equipment. Especially in a rapidly expanding church, one of the primary needs is for long-range planning. Suitable property must be located well in advance if growth is to be orderly, often before financing is available or thought to be remotely possible. This committee can offer invaluable assistance by helping the church make timely acquisitions of land and other needed facilities. Finally, most states have laws governing church corporations, which spell out certain legal responsibilities of trustees.

Personnel Committee

This committee is responsible for recommending staff salaries and fringe benefits. In addition, it should see that policies for vacations, sick leave, retirement, and bonuses are given in writing to each employee. As federal regulations become a reality in the area of pensions, it is important that someone be knowledgeable of current requirements and see that the church is in compliance. In the beginning stage, a small church may elect to have one or more members of the finance committee perform this function.

Pastor and Staff Members

In addition to the many duties of a minister, the pastor is frequently called upon to be the chief administrative officer. In financial matters the pastor should not (on a regular basis) be required to do any actual handling of cash. The pastor's primary responsibility in financial matters should be in emphasizing stewardship in both the giving and spending of resources. Unless the pastor appreciates the importance of having adequate controls and gives direction in financial matters, efforts by other employees and lay persons will be rendered somewhat ineffective.

Business Functions

The primary business functions that need to be recognized are discussed in the following topics: budget preparation, keeping of member records, separation of asset custody and record keeping, control over cash receipts, designating responsibility for disbursements, and reporting to membership.

Budget Preparation

Financial planning and control are difficult without a budget. Even the smallest church should have one. The budget may be viewed as a planning document that focuses on programs and needs for one or more years in advance. A budget forces the organization to anticipate both the inflow and outflow of funds. Assuming a limited amount of income, as is the case in most churches, the budget serves as an allocation device. Expenditures are directed toward specified needs and objectives. While the mechanics and details of budget preparation are covered in the next chapter, it should be observed here that the budget is a plan and is subject to change and revision to meet new program needs. The church should vote to adopt the budget initially and likewise should vote on any amendments changing the amounts and/or purposes for expenditures.

Member Records

Givers' records. Stewardship of both time and money is a highly personal matter. By maintaining an accurate record of member gifts and mailing a report periodically to its members, the church is fulfilling a fundamental stewardship responsibility. As illustrated in chapter 3, the record also serves as a reminder to members of their stewardship of money. The church's record of individual giving will also aid members in substantiating their tax deductions.

Pledge cards. A delicate and rather personal question a church must decide is whether to use pledge cards. Should church members be asked to make their intentions known in writing? Or is it sufficient to rely on past records of giving? While a number of successful churches do not ask members to sign pledge cards, there are perhaps more churches that do. One form of pledge card is presented in chapter 2. If pledge cards are used, a further question arises regarding follow-up action to see how the member is progressing. Does the church need to send a reminder of the pledge, giving progress to date? Here again the practice varies considerably. Each church should decide which policy is best. If the pledge is stated as a certain weekly or monthly amount, the average member probably does not need and would not appreciate a reminder. It is possible to send out quarterly statements of year-to-date giving and accomplish the same goal.

Offering envelopes. The church should give each member offering envelopes for the entire year. Each envelope is imprinted with a number as a means of more accurately identifying the gift and the giver. By having an envelope for each designated period in which gifts are received, the member is reminded of this responsibility. As explained in chapter 3, in the process of counting and depositing the receipts, the counters can compare to see that envelope amounts agree with the money given, thus providing a further check on accuracy.

Separation of Asset Custody and Record Keeping

A basic rule for financial control is to provide for the separation of actual asset custody and the keeping of the records. This procedure provides a cross-check on accountability and protects the custodian of the funds. For example, in retail establishments, cash is usually collected by store clerks who ring up the cash in a cash register. At the end of the day, the actual receipts are balanced against the register totals and sales tickets and turned over to a central cashier for deposit. The deposit record is then given to the bookkeeper-accountant who enters it in the books. With this separation of duties among several employees it would be unlikely that a loss or a theft of cash would go unnoticed.

In a small church it is difficult to build in "checks" and "balances." Even so, the finance committee, treasurer, and financial secretary should insist on cross-checks whenever possible. All disbursements should be made by checks that require two signatures. The person who countersigns should review invoices and other supporting documents. Control would further be strengthened by having a third person who is not a check signer prepare the monthly bank reconciliation. The reconciliation procedure should require that the paid check be compared with the disbursement record. An additional control procedure is to have someone perform periodically a post-audit either on a formal or informal basis. Some churches have their records audited regularly by an outside independent public accountant. In other cases, either a member of the finance committee or someone des-

ignated should perform a review of the receipts and disbursements. To reemphasize, a church should not turn all financial matters over to one individual. The church has a responsibility to persons in positions of trust to specify procedures that will provide some means of cross-checking. Such a policy is as much for the protection of the individual as for the church itself.

Cash Receipts

All cash receipts from whatever source should be deposited either daily or as often as needed. The receipts should be deposited intact without making any expenditures from those receipts. A better record is preserved if disbursements are made only by check or from an authorized petty cash fund established for that purpose. Funds in excess of normal day-to-day needs should be deposited in accounts to earn interest. Procedures relating to counting and depositing cash are discussed in chapter 3.

Responsibility for Disbursements

All expenditures must be approved by the church. Except for unexpected items that arise, most expenditures will be approved through the adoption of the church budget. While the budget sets a limit on amounts that may be expended for each major category, additional procedures are needed to coordinate the making of specific purchase commitments in these categories as well as the actual writing of checks for the purchases.

Many payments that must be made are for wages, utilities, and other items that recur on a weekly or monthly basis and do not require individual approval. Other payments for such items as supplies, equipment maintenance, and equipment need specific approval each time there is a payment. To be effective, control over disbursements for these items should begin before an actual purchase commitment is made. When a purchase is necessary, it may be initiated by the financial secretary, treasurer, finance committee chairperson, pastor, or the responsible department or organization leader. If the proposed expenditure has not been budgeted and is above a certain specified maximum, it must be presented for church approval. In fact, it is a good policy to require that non-recurring purchases over a stated maximum, say $500, be presented for church approval even though the item is budgeted. Another requirement should be that purchases at a lower level—for example, $250 or less—be approved by the finance committee chairperson, treasurer, or the department or organization leader involved. The fact that an item has been requested and included in the approved budget is not sufficient from a control standpoint. By requiring approval of large expenditures, there will be less room for criticism of the treasurer, pastor, and staff in the handling of funds. Further descriptions and illustrations of the disbursement process will be found in chapter 4.

Reporting to Membership

Reporting to the membership should be done on a regular basis, usually monthly. If members take an active part in the life of the church, they will be interested in and will want to know the church's financial progress. Members will be better able to determine and assess progress if both actual and budgeted amounts are reported. The reporting form as well as the extent of detail will vary among churches. In chapter 7, a reporting format is presented that may be adapted to fit the needs of almost any church.

Chapter 2
The Budget

This chapter is concerned with the budget as a useful device to aid in financial planning and to provide control. Churches have definite goals; therefore, they need a plan or budget to help prepare for financing the activities leading to the attainment of such goals. A budget requires considerable effort by the entire organization. In the process of preparing a budget, the church is forced to define certain categories and classifications for expenditures. Projected plans and programs must be converted into estimated dollar amounts. The same categories used in preparing the budget will also serve later when reporting on the utilization of resources. Actual results can be compared with budget estimates for each category, providing a means for evaluating performance.

A Word on Budgeting Philosophy

Ideas and questions abound as to the purpose and meaning of a budget. What is it? Who prepares it? What use is to be made of it? How much to budget? Without attempting a lengthy discussion of these and many similar questions, several statements are presented here to summarize the aspects of budgeting that are of special interest to churches.

1. Budget planning and preparation require input from the entire church organization. Either the finance committee or a church appointed budget planning committee should be responsible for coordinating the activity and presenting the budget for church approval. The treasurer should serve as a member of the finance and/or budget planning committee.

2. The church, in one or more business sessions, should have the opportunity to discuss the budget and vote on its adoption. Likewise, it should discuss and vote on subsequent amendments and changes of significance in amounts and/or purposes of expenditures.

3. As a practical matter, the budget will require careful planning of both programs and costs. An important question arises when considering the size of overall budget amounts, especially if receipts at the present level are likely to be below projected expenditures. Is it necessary to curtail planning for activities next year because funds were inadequate

this year? If growth is to take place and initiative to be encouraged, at least while the budget is being planned, then persons responsible for achieving the organizations' goals and objectives should be encouraged to think in terms of programs that are needed. It may be possible that planned programs will generate new interest and thereby encourage members to increase their giving. Thus, worthwhile goals may be achieved that otherwise would not be considered.

Organizational leaders, including the pastor and church staff, should be requested, when planning, to set a priority or ranking for their programs. Later, if it is necessary to reduce budget requests, lower priority programs can be scaled down first.

4. Provision should be made for unexpected needs that arise during the year after the budget has been approved. If evolving programs require only small amounts, these changes can usually be covered by specifying a small sum for such contingencies in the original budget. Any large amounts should be presented for church approval. A budget that does not allow some flexibility is not realistic and may be impossible to live with.

5. While the church should engage in long-range plans involving more than one year, this chapter is primarily concerned with the budget for a single year.

6. The church should adopt a timetable for accomplishing the budget-planning cycle. This topic is discussed in the section that follows.

Steps in the Budgeting Process

As stated above, a timetable including all the necessary steps in the entire budgeting process should be approved by the church. Once approved, the same basic process would be repeated each year. While in our discussion the fiscal period is assumed to be the calendar year, it could be any twelve-month period. The following suggestions are applicable to the entire cycle and give time periods to accomplish it.

1. Set date for first meeting of finance or budget planning committee to discuss plans for the coming year. Assuming that newly elected church officers and department leaders

begin their term of office in September, the meeting should be held in early August.

2. Request projections for next year's budget from pastor and organizational leaders. All projections should be completed by the end of September. When making requests, the budget planning committee should provide necessary details of actual expenditures for the past year.

3. After requests are collected and compiled, the entire committee should meet (early in October) to discuss and approve the budget. In some cases, church bylaws may require that a designated board consider and approve the budget before it is presented to the church. In this event, a second or combined meeting should be held of this board and the budget planning committee. At this meeting there should be an opportunity to raise questions and to make suggestions as to any budget item.

4. Following approval, but prior to discussion in the business session, a copy of the recommended budget should be mailed or otherwise distributed to every church member.

5. Next, the budget should be presented and discussed in church business meeting. Any proposed amendments should be discussed, allowing the department or organization concerned to present any needed explanations.

6. Amendments should be compiled by the budget planning committee and the budget presented for adoption at either a regularly scheduled or a specially called business meeting.

7. Following adoption of the budget, a copy should be mailed to members. If pledge cards are to be used, they should be mailed at this time. The procedure at this point will vary depending on how much emphasis is to be placed on obtaining pledges and whether the church conducts some kind of every member canvass. One approach is an all-out effort led primarily by lay persons to visit in the home of every church member. These visits can be very beneficial in a number of ways. They can lead to increased participation and a renewal of interest by the members in the overall church program. When members become interested and involved, they will likely want to support the church financially. The result of each visit may be to obtain a signed pledge card; however, it may be preferable to leave the pledge cards with the members and request that they turn them in on pledge day. An alternative approach to that of visiting in the home of each member would be to visit only the members who do not return a pledge card during the pledge period. Another possibility would be to have the church members march down the aisle on pledge day during the worship service and give their pledge cards. Follow-up action would be necessary for return of pledge cards by members who were not present.

8. If pledges are adequate to support the budget, no further action is necessary. However, if after follow-up the pledges are inadequate, it may be necessary to revise the budget downward. The finance and budget planning committee should be charged with the responsibility of scaling down the budget items according to the priorities established earlier by organizational directors and leaders. In some cases, the organizational leaders and other persons making the requests will need to be consulted before changes are made.

The Process Illustrated

An established church should have already a list of budget or expenditure accounts. If so, the budget accounts should be reviewed and changed as necessary to reflect current programs and requirements. On the other hand, a new church must develop a list of accounts from scratch. Since the budget accounts also serve as categories for recording the actual expenditures as they occur, care must be taken at this stage to include all the accounts that will be needed throughout the year. Exhibit 2-1 is a budget worksheet with all the accounts needed for a small to medium-sized church.

In order to demonstrate the practical aspects of budget preparation and subsequent reporting, assumed information is presented on this form for Sample Church. It includes columns for actual results for the most recent eight months (column 1), budget for current year (column 2), amounts requested for next year (column 3), and amounts recommended for next year's budget (column 4). The worksheet is shown in its completed form and will be referred to throughout the discussion. Preparation of reports in chapter 7 is based on the same budget accounts and amounts.

1. To initiate the process, the budget planning committee should make budget requests of each organizational director, the pastor, and any person responsible for programs and activities. While it is unnecessary to follow a rigid format, information similar to that in Exhibit 2-2 should be included as part of the request procedure.

Before the forms are distributed, the budget planning committee should fill in the first two columns showing the budget for the year and actual year-to-date expenditures. While this data is not illustrated here, it might be helpful to some of the program directors to provide actual data for the most recent twelve-month period. Also, it may be necessary for some activities to give year-to-date actual results coupled with projected expenditures for the months remaining to arrive at a more realistic basis for projections. In our example amounts shown for 8 months would be multiplied by the fraction 12/8, to give the projected amount for 12 months. This approach may be helpful especially in the face of rising prices along with rapid growth in membership and other factors causing expenditure increases.

Organizational directors and other persons in leadership roles need complete budget information and should also be given a copy of the budget worksheet at the time they are given their budget request form. At this time the budget

EXHIBIT 2-1
SAMPLE CHURCH BUDGET WORKSHEET
For Budget Period January 1, 1980 through December 31, 1980

Account Number	Account	(1) Actual for most recent 8 months	(2) Budget for current year	(3) Budget Requests for next year (see notes)	(4) Budget recommended for next year
201	BUDGET RECEIPTS (a)	$39,000	$60,000	_____	$65,000
	DISBURSEMENTS:				
	Missions (b)				
301	Denominational	5,850	9,000	9,750	9,750
302	Local	320	400	450	450
303	Other	150	300	320	320
	Total	6,320	9,700	10,520	10,520
	Educational Ministry (c)				
401	Literature, materials, and supplies	1,260	1,600	1,750	1,750
402	Women's mission and auxiliaries	420	600	600	600
403	Brotherhood and auxiliaries	405	600	670	670
404	Music and choirs	955	1,200	1,350	1,350
405	College and youth	610	800	800	800
406	Library	165	200	240	240
	Total	3,815	5,000	5,410	5,410
	Personnel Salaries & Allowances (d)				
501	Pastor	10,000	15,000	16,050	16,050
502	Minister of youth and music	1,000	1,200	1,200	1,200
503	Church secretary	4,800	7,200	7,705	7,705
504	Janitorial	800	1,400	1,500	1,500
505	Part-time help	45	200	200	200
	Total	16,645	25,000	26,655	26,655
	General Operations				
601	Office supplies and bulletins (e)	1,250	1,900	2,140	2,140
602	Postage (e)	605	850	950	950
603	Utilities (e)	2,310	3,600	3,960	3,960
604	Telephone (e)	502	720	850	850
605	Property insurance (f)	350	650	680	680
606	Kitchen (c)	608	900	1,050	1,050
607	Car allowance and mileage (d)	2,450	2,600	2,800	2,800
608	Conventions and conferences (g)	345	500	540	540
609	Hospital insurance and retirement (d)	968	1,452	1,520	1,520
610	F.I.C.A. tax expenses (d)	288	432	510	510
611	Publicity, advertising, and promotion (c)	272	360	400	400
612	Flowers, decorations (c)	206	300	330	330
613	Other—contingency	408	936	—	985
	Total	10,562	15,200	15,730	16,715
	Property and Equipment (f)				
701	Maintenance—building and grounds	700	1,000	1,100	1,100
702	Maintenance—office and other	868	1,300	1,500	1,500
703	Equipment purchases	900	1,200	1,500	1,500
	Total	2,468	3,500	4,100	4,100
801	Debt Retirement (f)	1,200	1,600	1,600	1,600
	Total	$41,010	$60,000	$64,015	$65,000

[Explanations of notes (a) through (g) follow.]

NOTE: Sample figures throughout this revised edition are unchanged from the original and are for illustration only. They are not intended to suggest actual budgets.

Footnotes to Budget Worksheet

(a) Budget receipts. Total budget receipts are usually equal to the total of expenditures in the approved budget. This equality results in a "balanced" budget.

(b) Missions requests are the responsibility of the missions committee.

(c) Amounts for educational ministry, including training materials, auxiliaries, music, youth and library needs, would be provided by the organizational directors/leaders in conjunction with the pastor and staff.

(d) Personnel committee should make all recommendations as to salaries, allowances, benefits, and payroll taxes.

(e) Budget planning committee should make estimates, based upon revision of past actual amounts, for such items as office supplies, utilities, postage, and other similar items.

(f) Trustees should give assistance in budgeting for property, equipment, and debt retirement.

(g) Pastor will submit request for conventions and conferences and, in addition, will give direction to organizational leaders in making their requests.

worksheet (Exhibit 2-1) will have only the first two columns completed. But this information will enable them to see their requests and the overall budget in proper perspective. For this reason, as suggested earlier and further illustrated in chapter 7 on reporting, both actual and budget data should be reported periodically, either monthly or quarterly, to the entire church. In addition, as a basis for preparing their estimates for next year, some directors will need additional detail of prior periods, showing vendors to whom the payments were made.

2. For each account included on the budget worksheet, the budget committee should identify the organization or person responsible to provide budget data. Even in smaller churches, most of the budget requests will be made by lay persons in leadership positions after consultation with the pastor and staff. In the worksheet for Sample Church, Exhibit 2-1, the person responsible for each account is identified by using notes (a) through (g). In actual practice, the notes should be attached to the worksheet and distributed during the budget-planning process.

3. After budget requests are collected, the amounts are posted on the worksheet in column 3. The completed postings are shown in Exhibit 2-1, a total for all categories of $64,015. Next, the budget planning committee must enter in column 4 the recommended amounts for next year's budget. At this point there is some difference of opinion as to the proper function of the committee. Does the committee have authority to impose fiscal restraint and perhaps set guidelines for requests in the budget-planning stage? Or should it simply tabulate requests and present them to the church in final form without making recommendations? Questions of this nature need to be answered before the process begins, preferably at the beginning of each budget cycle and perhaps even in the constitution and bylaws. It would be impossible here to give an answer that would adequately describe the role of this committee to fit all churches and all situations.

For example, a church faced with declining enrollment and member contributions with no prospects for improvement in the near term already has a severe constraint placed

EXHIBIT 2-2
BUDGET REQUEST FORM

Budget Request Form

TO: Pastor, departmental officers, trustees, personnel committee, missions committee, auxiliaries, etc.

FROM: Budget planning committee

Please complete the information requested below and submit it by Sept. 30, 1979 _____ :

Account Number	Account Name	For Current Budget Period		Budget Request for 1980
		Budget for year	Actual for 8 months to date	
301	Denominational Missions	$9,000	$5,850	15% of budget receipts
302	Local Missions	400	320	450
303	Other (please list)	300	150	320
	Totals	$9,700	$6,320	$

In the space below, give as much information as possible in support of your request, including a breakdown of each account according to functions, programs, activities, costs, etc. Also, to help the budget committee in the event budget revisions are necessary, identify which programs have first priority and which can be reduced or curtailed, giving amounts involved where possible.

_____

_____

_____

Please write on the reverse side of this form equipment needs or other major expenditures that will arise in the near future—a want list.

---

on next year's budget requests. At the other extreme, a growing church with seemingly unlimited potential for growth in enrollment must seek to provide programs and activities that will further such growth despite a lack of demonstrated financial support. For a church that continues at somewhat the same level of membership, the budget would tend to be fairly constant except for increases in costs due to rising prices. In most cases, as a minimum the committee should be charged with the responsibility of reviewing budget requests and, by discussion with departmental officers and other responsible persons, determining that requests are supported by programs and activities that are appropriate and in keeping with the church's objectives. Requests for amounts that appear to be clearly out of line with current levels of giving should be identified and any differences of opinion resolved before the final budget is compiled.

In our example the recommended budget for Sample Church, shown in column 4 of Exhibit 2-1, totals $65,000. The only change by the budget committee was to add a small amount for contingencies, $985 in account 613. While it is not essential to round the budget to the nearest thousand, the Sample Church committee did so and added perhaps a little more to the account than will be needed.

4. After distributing the recommended budget to church members for their consideration, the budget should be presented by the budget committee at the monthly business meeting or a called meeting. The committee should explain the budget in overall terms, giving sufficient information to account for the major changes in amounts and programs from the prior year without going into each account in detail. For example, increases in personnel salaries and benefits would usually be the result of factors such as cost of living adjustments, merit increases, and changes in personnel. An increase in postage would be due to higher postal rates and/or increased mailings. An alternative approach followed in some churches is to have organizational leaders present their sections of the budget or at least be prepared to offer explanations if questions are raised by the congregation. After compiling the recommendations and changes suggested and approved by the membership, a final draft should be prepared and distributed to all members. In our example, since the church did not recommend any changes, the copy to be sent to members would include the amounts shown in column 4. The information in the first three columns, while useful in the planning stages, should not be included.

5. Several factors should be considered in planning the final meeting to approve the budget. To achieve maximum publicity for the financial aspects of the church program, the meeting should be at a time when attendance is highest, usually at a morning worship service. Since the members have already had an opportunity to discuss the budget and

to vote on changes, at the final meeting the church should vote to approve or disapprove the entire budget without further discussion. If the budget does in fact receive approval of a large percentage of church members, such widespread show of support should help in obtaining pledges from the membership. Of course there is always the possibility that the church will vote to disapprove the budget. In this case several of the above steps must be repeated to make any needed amendments.

6. After the budget has been approved, the budget committee should attempt to determine the support that members are willing to give. In one church that has exceptional financial support, members are asked to prove their level of support for one week by demonstrated giving. This is done near the end of the old budget year. While some churches depend on their members to give without making specific pledges, many find pledge cards to be helpful. As dicussed above, if some type of every member canvass is to be undertaken, plans should be made and advance publicity given when the members receive their pledge cards. When the members are aware that an effort is being made by their church to secure pledge cards from everyone, they will usually be more inclined to return them during the pledge period. An effective promotional campaign telling about the budget and how amounts are to be spent is essential before distributing pledge cards. Special programs and materials should be designed to provide this emphasis. If the members are made fully aware of proposed programs and activities, they should feel more personally involved and want to pledge at a higher level. The pledge card should be as simple as possible. As shown in Exhibit 2-3, the member's pledge can be stated in weekly, monthly, or annual amounts.

On the date designated as pledge day, every member should be encouraged to bring a pledge card. Promotional material should stress the importance of every member participation and of reaching this goal as well as the monetary goal the first day. As a climax to the worship service on pledge day, both the number of pledges and the amount pledged should be announced. Several members of the finance committee should be on hand to tabulate the results. For later follow-up, it will be helpful to indicate on the membership roster members who returned a pledge card. At some point the pledge cards should be arranged in alphabetical order.

Also, a course of action should be decided by the church in the event that the budget is either oversubscribed or undersubscribed. Pledges in excess of the budget may permit revisions to include programs or other items that were being delayed. If the pledges made plus the demonstrated giving potential of members not pledging is considered inadequate to support the proposed budget, revisions should be made by eliminating programs having the lowest priority. Ideally, a workable budget will result from this revision,

EXHIBIT 2-3
PLEDGE CARD

Sample Church—Pledge Card for the _____ Budget Year

Your name:_____

In support of our financial program for the coming year, I anticipate that I will give as follows (check *one* and fill in the appropriate amounts):

(   ) A tithe of my income. My estimated gift on a weekly basis $_____; on a monthly basis $_____; on an annual basis $_____. (You need fill in only one of the three amounts.)

(   ) I will give $_____ (per week) (per month) (per year).

(   ) I do not wish to pledge a definite amount but will give as I am able.

making it unnecessary to request action by the church throughout the year each time a significant expenditure is proposed.

If the church has not made an effort to contact members prior to this time, perhaps such a plan should be considered. While the financial goal of pledging the budget amount is important, some churches prefer to emphasize the goal of every member participation, assuming that by reaching this goal, the church will also attain the financial goal. As suggested earlier, one course of action would be to contact by telephone or personal visit members who do not return their cards. At the minimum, mail reminders should be sent to members who do not make a pledge during the pledge period.

Chapter 3
Cash Receipts

This chapter presents procedures designed (1) to accomplish the necessary record keeping for cash receipts and (2) to help provide essential checks and balances. As stated earlier, control over cash requires separation of duties so that no one individual has complete charge over deposits or transactions from beginning to end. In small churches with few, if any, full-time employees, it is difficult to achieve separation of duties, thus necessitating some additional steps to make up for this weakness. While the following discussion emphasizes specific steps in the cash-receiving process, the steps are designed to implement control procedures.

Cash is received at a number of different times and from a number of different sources, such as the following:

- By passing of collection plates among the congregation during regular worship services.

- From the offering given by the Sunday church school classes and other groups meeting for Bible study.

- At weekly church suppers, banquets, and other occasions when members pay for their meals.

- Mail receipts that come to the church for both regular and designated purposes.

- Occasional sale of books and literature to members.

- Special fund-raising efforts through sale of bonds, member solicitation for building programs, etc.

As cash is received, regardless of the timing or source, it must be carefully protected and accounted for to assure that it goes for the purpose intended by the donor. Essential steps in controlling and recording cash receipts include the following:

- Count the cash, recording the total for later comparison with the deposit record.

- Prepare a report of deposit, giving an adequate breakdown of receipts (between undesignated and designated gifts) for later recording in the journal.

- Deposit the receipts in a bank, daily where possible.

- Maintain a record of gifts for each donor.

- From the report of deposit enter summary totals in the receipts journal.

- Prepare for membership periodic reports showing amounts contributed broken down into major categories.

While the above procedures may appear to be excessive, keep in mind that desired accuracy can be achieved only by timely counting and safeguarding receipts. In the remaining pages of this chapter each of the above steps is described in greater detail.

Counting of Receipts

As a matter of church policy, members of the finance committee, the treasurer, designated counters, or other appointed persons should be responsible for receiving collections of cash and other gifts. The actual counting procedure should first verify the amount and donor so that giving records may be updated. The entire process is made easier if individual offering envelopes are provided. An example is provided in Exhibit 3-1.

These special envelopes are widely used for a number of reasons, one of which is the promotion of stewardship. Members and others who wish to give should be provided with envelopes for use each week. For control and accuracy in identifying givers, the envelopes should be prenumbered. An alphabetical list of members with their assigned numbers will be helpful when an envelope is received without a name. In addition to regular envelopes, special envelopes should be printed for offerings received for designated causes, such as missions and building-fund drives. Such envelopes are not usually prenumbered, but having an easily identifiable envelope makes for more accuracy in keeping up with designated gifts as well as promoting the offering cause.

When receipts are collected during regular worship, as well as during Sunday church school or Bible study periods,

EXHIBIT 3-1
OFFERING ENVELOPE

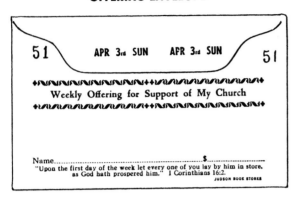

ushers, organizational leaders, class secretaries, and others who receive collections should immediately turn them over to a designated person or persons. At this point the practice varies somewhat depending on when the counting is to be done, who is to do the actual counting, and when the bank deposit is to be made. Control procedures are described for three situations, as follows: (*a*) in smaller churches, when the treasurer will take the collections home and deposit them within the week; (*b*) in some churches where the day's collections are left in an overnight vault and counted by church staff members the next day; or (*c*) in larger churches where the procedure is for one or more members to count and deposit the collection as soon as it is received.

Procedures for counting and depositing in smaller churches should be kept as simple as possible. The person who serves as organizational secretary should total the gifts received through the Sunday church school classes before turning them over to the treasurer. In many churches this is routinely done and a report is made to the membership during the morning worship hour. While the treasurer may wish to add the amounts and agree to the total before taking custody of the receipts from Sunday church school, this step would not appear to be essential. Collections made during the morning worship hour present a slightly different problem. If at all possible someone should count the receipts and obtain a total before giving them to the treasurer. One of the ushers could be designated to count the loose coins and currency and make a tape or pencil list of the envelopes without actually opening them and removing the contents. Since each situation is somewhat unique, it is difficult to suggest an approach that best suits every church. However, totals for both Sunday church school and the morning worship should be retained by someone in the church office for later use by the finance committee. The actual procedures for counting, depositing, and preparing the report of deposit by the treasurer is presented following the next section.

Consider next the procedures for churches that leave their collections overnight in a vault or safe to be counted by church staff members the following day. Here as well as in the first case, the amount of the collections should be determined before leaving them for someone else to count and deposit. A total of the collections received through Sunday church school classes is usually obtained as soon as the class records and envelopes are returned to the department or general secretary. This total will be used later by the finance committee for comparison purposes. Also, collections during the morning worship period should be added and a total determined. All that is necessary here is to prepare an adding machine tape of the envelope amounts and of the total loose coins and currency. At least two persons should be designated for this task. It would be possible to utilize two of the ushers or else one of the ushers and maybe the financial secretary, church treasurer, or a member of the finance committee. While a certain amount of effort is essential to obtain these totals, without them control over cash receipts will not be adequate. The actual process of opening envelopes, counting, preparation of the deposit slip, and a report of deposit will be the same as that described in the next section where the deposit is made by the counting committee on the day it is collected.

Control procedures can be more easily accomplished in larger churches. Since most collections are received on Sunday, the counting should be done immediately. This means that members who serve as counters will be unable to participate in regular church activities. For this reason counters should be rotated frequently, counting at most only one Sunday each month. Control is enhanced by having at least two people each time to do the counting. The following procedures should be followed regardless of when the actual count is made.

1. As the contents are removed from the envelope, determine that the actual gift agrees with the amount specified by the giver on the outside. If found to be in agreement, make a notation on the envelope by a check mark; or, even better, circle the amount. In the example below, Exhibit 3-2, observe that the amount can be easily identified for later posting.

EXHIBIT 3-2
OFFERING ENVELOPE
AS MARKED

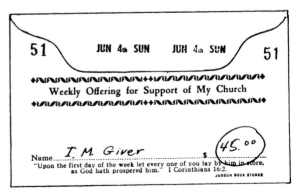

If no amount has been specified on the envelope or if the amount does not agree with the actual gift, the counter should mark through the incorrect amount and fill in the correct amount and either circle or otherwise identify it. Unless the amount of the gift is clearly established at this point, it will be impossible to make an accurate posting later to the giver's record. It will also be impossible to balance later the actual currency, coins, and checks with the envelope totals.

2. Equally as important as the amount is to establish the name of the donor. A gift by check is easy to verify by comparing the check with the envelope. If the donor did not write his or her name on the outside, this should be done by the counter. Occasionally, an envelope that contains cash will not have a name, presenting a different problem. If a record is kept of envelope numbers assigned to members, these envelopes can be checked against the alphabetical list. As a last resort, it may be necessary to contact the member to clear up any question about a specific gift or envelope. It is most important to have a name so that the member's record can be posted. If the counter is unable to determine the donor when a cash gift is involved, the amount should be counted in with loose collections. Frequently the donor, in making a gift by check, will do so without using an envelope. In this case the counter must prepare an envelope, writing on it the donor's name, amount of the gift, and any other information which is specified on the check.

3. Counters should determine if the gift is undesignated in nature or whether it is intended by the donor for a specific cause. While it is recommended that specially prepared envelopes be used for designated gifts, such as for fund drives and mission causes, members will often include these amounts with their regular offering. The amount so designated is usually written by the donor either on the envelope, on the check itself, or both. Counters have little difficulty if only a few such envelopes are received. However, if a large number are involved, the counter should prepare a separate envelope for the designated portion of the check, making certain that the name and amount are correct. After making a new envelope for the designated portion, verify that the total undesignated and designated amounts equal the amount of the check.

4. After the checks have been removed, they should be endorsed with the restrictive endorsement "for deposit only," followed by the name of the church. Enter checks on the deposit slip by amount and donor's last name. While the deposit slip should not be used to make the postings to givers' records, having the name on the deposit slip is often helpful later when questions arise in posting from the envelopes. Count the coins and currency and enter totals on the deposit slip. As seen in Exhibit 3-3, the deposit slip is completed by entering the deposit total.

EXHIBIT 3-3
DEPOSIT SLIP

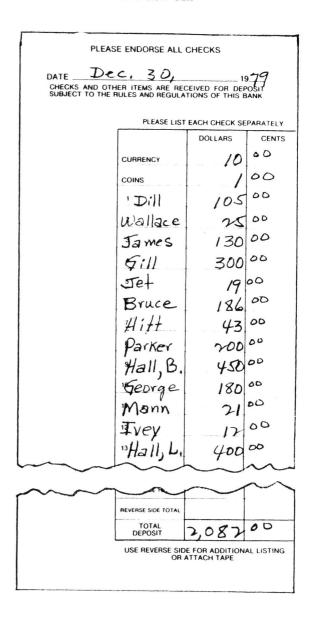

PLEASE ENDORSE ALL CHECKS		
DATE _Dec. 30,_____ 19_79_		
CHECKS AND OTHER ITEMS ARE RECEIVED FOR DEPOSIT SUBJECT TO THE RULES AND REGULATIONS OF THIS BANK		
PLEASE LIST EACH CHECK SEPARATELY	DOLLARS	CENTS
CURRENCY	10	00
COINS	1	00
¹ Dill	105	00
Wallace	25	00
James	130	00
Gill	300	00
Jet	19	00
Bruce	186	00
Hitt	43	00
Parker	700	00
Hall, B.	450	00
George	180	00
Mann	21	00
Ivey	17	00
¹³ Hall, L.	400	00
REVERSE SIDE TOTAL		
TOTAL DEPOSIT	2,082	00
USE REVERSE SIDE FOR ADDITIONAL LISTING OR ATTACH TAPE		

Prepare Report of Deposit

At this point enter the detail from the deposit slip on the report of deposit illustrated in Exhibit 3-4. In the spaces provided, enter total of checks, currency, and coins. Some counters may prefer to enter the count of coins and currency on the report of deposit and later transfer it onto the deposit slip. When added together, these amounts should agree with the deposit slip total. If they agree, you may assume the deposit is correct. In our example, the deposit total is $2,082.

The next step is to add the amounts on the envelopes and enter the totals on the report of deposit by undesignated and

EXHIBIT 3-4
REPORT OF DEPOSIT

Date <u>Dec. 30, 1979</u> Counted by <u>Appleton and Travis</u>

Envelope Summary

General budget:

Envelope total	$1,781.00
Loose collections	11.00
Total	1,792.00

Designated gifts:

Building fund	200.00
Organ fund	
Other:	
Wedding (for building use)	10.00
Kitchen receipts	80.00
Total envelopes	$2,082.00

Deposit Summary

Total checks			$2,071.00
Currency:	$1	10.00	
	$5		
	Other		
	$.01		10.00
Coins:	.05		
	.10		
	.25	1.00	
	.50		1.00
Total deposit			$2,082.00

---

designated categories. Loose collections not in envelopes were $11 in total. Finally, add the report and compare the total envelope summary with the deposit total. Are they in agreement? If so, consider that you have had a good day. If not, go back over the tape of envelopes and try to figure out where the error occurred. Assuming that you have added the report and the checks correctly, you will find the envelopes as the most likely source of error. When you opened the envelope, did you see that the envelope amount was the same as the contents removed? In most cases if you review each one, in the process you will be able to recall or otherwise determine how the error occurred. Remember also that the names of those giving by check are on the

deposit slip, facilitating a quick comparison with the envelopes.

Carry Deposit to Bank

As soon as the counting has been completed and the deposit slip prepared, the deposit should be taken to the bank. Most banks provide a small locking canvas bag that can be dropped by access through a locked opening into the bank's vault. In this case, it will be necessary to go by and pick up the bag before making the next deposit. While it is not recommended that the deposit be left overnight in the church or taken home by the treasurer or a church member, in some cases there is no other alternative. If a

EXHIBIT 3-5
MEMBER CONTRIBUTION RECORD

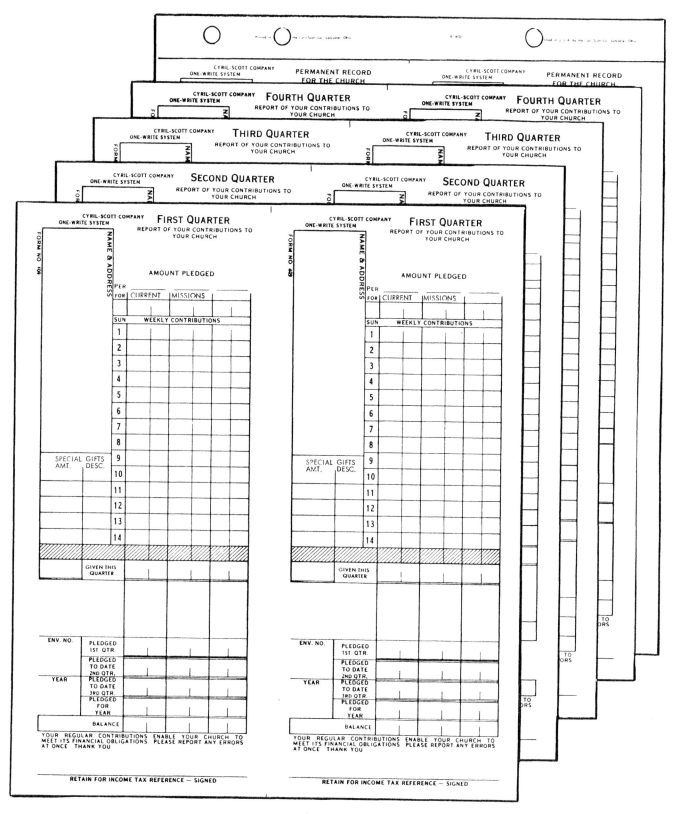

21

large amount is involved, it should be taken to the bank without exception. But regardless of the amount, proper control can be exercised only if the deposit total has been determined before any funds are removed from the church premises.

Record of Member Giving

With as little delay as possible, the member's giving record should be posted. While the format of the record may vary, space should be included for certain basic information including (*a*) member's name, (*b*) date the gift was received, (*c*) amount of gift, and (*d*) whether a gift was designated or undesignated. Exhibit 3-5 includes the above data and also provides quarterly and annual totals.

Before any posting is done to giving records, the envelopes should be placed in alphabetical order. After the posting has been completed, as a check on accuracy add from the givers' records the amounts actually posted. Make certain this total agrees with the amount on the report of deposit. While it may be unnecessary to prove the postings each week, it should be done at least quarterly as well as annually.

The frequency of mailing contribution records to members is a matter of church policy. At most the mailing would be done quarterly and at least annually. A number of other possibilities may be considered. For example, one church mails a copy after the November postings have been completed to give the member a year-to-date record. With this information the member will be able to determine the amount to be given in December to complete the amount pledged. Remember that giving records are highly personal, and extreme care should be exercised to keep them confidential.

Record Deposit in Cash Journal

The report of deposit provides a summary of each bank deposit and the necessary detail for reporting to the church membership. But before the financial reports can be prepared, information from each deposit must be further summarized and totals obtained. The journal provides this summary information. Each report of deposit is written in the journal. The journal that is illustrated in chapter 6 is designed to combine cash receipts and cash disbursements. In larger churches with many activities to account for, a separate cash receipts journal should be maintained to reduce the number of individual postings. Individual items on the report of deposit for December 30, 1979, shown earlier as Exhibit 3-4, are posted on one or more lines of the journal. Further explanation of the journal is offered in chapter 4 in the discussion of cash disbursements.

Reporting to Membership

Most churches prepare for the membership a monthly financial report combining both cash receipts and disbursements. As illustrated in the reports prepared in chapter 7, receipts are presented by major categories including designated and undesignated gifts. Undesignated gifts need to be shown only as a single amount. Designated gifts are given in further detail depending on the nature of the gifts and the amount involved.

Chapter 4
Cash Disbursements

This chapter presents a method for controlling disbursements in accord with the established budget. Overall guidelines for the making of disbursements and suggested procedures will be outlined. The use of the checkbook to provide a basis for record keeping will be described. Chapter 5 will then outline general accounting procedures, and chapter 6 will show how receipts and disbursements are recorded in the journal and then posted to the ledger.

Overall Procedures for Disbursements

The church should adopt a set of policies that specify both authority and responsibility for making expenditures. At the minimum, the constitution or bylaws should define who is to keep the records and how disbursements are to be made, including the necessary levels of approval for disbursement requests. In general, the church should adopt a policy that will make it as simple as possible to make disbursements for normal, recurring items and yet retain final say over unusual items that arise infrequently. Embodied in the statements below are financial matters that should be considered in drafting church policies and procedures for making disbursements.

1. As discussed in chapter 2 on budgeting, insofar as possible, disbursements should be provided for in a church-approved budget. Church approval should also be required for expenditures not currently budgeted; however, the treasurer and finance committee, at their discretion, should be authorized to make adjustments and transfers within budget accounts except for salaries and allowances, debt retirement, and missions, all of which should require church approval. Some flexibility in spending is necessary, or else the church as a whole will be constantly involved in trivial matters. Amounts provided for in the approved budget should be disbursed according to certain guidelines such as the following:

a. Approval of the treasurer only should be required for payment of items over which there is little discretion or control as to the amount or payee, such as principal and interest payments on church indebtedness; salaries, allowances, and related payroll taxes; utilities and insur-

ance; mission causes whether a budget specified amount or based on a percentage of current budget receipts; other budgeted amounts under a certain specified minimum (e.g., $50).

b. In addition to the treasurer, organizational directors must approve expenditures made for their specific programs. Such expenditures in excess of a certain maximum (e.g., $250) should require approval at a higher level, such as by the deacons or trustees, and if in excess of a still larger specified maximum (e.g., $1,000) approval at an even higher level, perhaps by a vote of the church as a whole.

2. The treasurer (or chairperson of the finance committee in larger churches) should be responsible for seeing that disbursements are made according to church policy. The treasurer (with assistance from the financial secretary) will write the checks and keep all necessary records.

3. The treasurer with the cooperation and support of organizational leaders will seek to keep requests for disbursements in line with cash on hand and with current receipts. To maintain an adequate cash reserve may necessitate deferring expenditures which are othewise well within the budget.

4. Checks are to be signed by any two of the following: treasurer, chairperson of finance committee, chairperson of deacons, or a designated trustee.

5. Gifts of a designated nature may be disbursed with the treasurer's approval.

6. All disbursements should be made by check. In addition, some churches keep a small petty cash fund which is established by writing a check on the general account, cashing it and placing the funds with a designated person. This fund is subsequently reimbursed, when the funds have been expended, by writing a check payable to the petty cash custodian for the amounts disbursed, thereby restoring it to the original balance.

Requests for Disbursements

Throughout this chapter illustrations will refer to the budget accounts introduced in chapter 2 (see Exhibit 2-1).

Since the list is the subject of much of our discussion it is reproduced below.

EXHIBIT 4-1
CHART OF BUDGET ACCOUNTS

Account Number	Account
201	BUDGET RECEIPTS
	DISBURSEMENTS:
	Missions
301	Denominational
302	Local
303	Other
	Educational Ministry
401	Literature, materials, and supplies
402	Women's mission and auxiliaries
403	Brotherhood and auxiliaries
404	Music and choirs
405	College and youth
406	Library
	Personnel Salaries and Allowances
501	Pastor
502	Minister of youth and music
503	Church secretary
504	Janitorial
505	Part-time help
	General Operations
601	Office supplies and bulletins
602	Postage
603	Utilities
604	Telephone
605	Property insurance
606	Kitchen
607	Car allowance and mileage
608	Conventions and conferences
609	Hospital insurance and retirement
610	F.I.C.A. tax expense
611	Publicity, advertising, and promotion
612	Flowers, decorations
613	Other—contingency
	Property and Equipment
701	Maintenance—building and grounds
702	Maintenance—office and other
703	Equipment purchases
801	Debt Retirement

Before making a disbursement, assuming money is in the checking account, someone must determine whether the proposed expenditure is authorized and within the specified budget account to be charged. Payments of salaries, allowances, and principal and interest on debt are contractual in nature and usually are fixed annual amounts. For items of this type the total sum budgeted is divided into twelve equal amounts and paid each month. As stated above, such disbursements may be made by the treasurer (or financial secretary) and should not require any further approval. Also, payments made for utilities, including telephone, gas, electricity, and water, while they are not fixed annual amounts, are somewhat contractual in nature and should not require further approval. Even if the budget amount is exceeded, these payments are nondiscretionary, and approval at a higher level should not be necessary. The only approval needed should be that of the treasurer. Expenditures for most of the other budget items are somewhat discretionary and should require approval by organizational leaders and others responsible at the time that purchases are made.

In larger churches formal purchase orders may be required when ordering supplies and requesting services, but smaller churches will probably find purchase orders unnecessary. However, requests for purchases and other expenditures need to be properly approved to prevent overspending the budget. When prior approval is necessary, it should be obtained in writing to provide documentation when the check is written to the vendor. A form for this purpose is illustrated in Exhibit 4-2.

Space is provided on the form for such information as the payee's name and address, date payment is to be made, budget account to be charged, explanation of request, and person or persons approving it. In most cases the organizational leader will prepare and sign the form at the time a decision is made to spend budgeted funds. Before approval is given by the treasurer (or financial secretary), the request must be reviewed to see that it is within the budget allowance and also that funds are available. Especially if large amounts are involved as in the case of substantial purchases of equipment, the treasurer must determine that the cash flow will be adequate to cover required expenditures for nondiscretionary items like utilities and loan payments that may be due currently or in the near future.

Following is a summary, by budget categories for accounts, that illustrates when a disbursement request form would normally be required:

Budget Account or Category	Is a disbursement request form needed?	
	Yes	No
Missions		X
Educational ministry (all accounts)	X	
Personnel—salaries and allowances		X
Part-time help	X	
General operations		
Utilities, telephone, etc.		X
All other accounts	X	
Property and equipment— maintenance and purchase, all accounts	X	
Debt retirement		X

EXHIBIT 4-2
SAMPLE CHURCH
DISBURSEMENT REQUISITION

Date when payment
is needed:_____19_____   No._____

Purpose of   (1) If for a budget item: Account Number _____Account Name_____
disbursement: (2) If for designated item, identify donor or source_____
                 (3) Other (explain):_____

Make payment to:
(give address
where necessary)

Date	Enter description if invoice or other support is not attached or otherwise available. For travel, enter purpose and mileage.	Amount
Total		$

Signature of organizational director (where applicable):

Signature of person requesting travel reimbursement:

Approved:_____ (If over $)
          Chairperson, Finance Committee

(This space to be completed by financial sec'y)
Invoice checked for accuracy and price

Approved:_____ (If over $)
          Next higher level

Goods or services received_____

Approved:_____ (If over $)
          Church Clerk

Date paid_____ 19_____

Reviewed by audit committee_____

Check number _____

After a check has been written in payment of the disbursement requested, the Disbursement Requisition should be filed, usually in check number order. Vendor invoices and other documents should be attached and the date paid and check number entered in the spaces provided.

While a church should not become involved in unnecessary paperwork, it is essential that every disbursement have proper support. The purpose of specific rules and procedures should always be to make it possible to accomplish defined goals and objectives and avoid waste.

Forms for Checks

Two styles of checks are illustrated at the end of this chapter. Presented first in Exhibit 4-3 is the traditional check attached to a stub. Each time a check is written, the date, payee, and description must be entered on the stub. This dual writing can be avoided by using the voucher check form illustrated in Exhibit 4-4.

The voucher check form should consist of an original and one or more copies. Space is provided above the check to write a description of the payment. The copy retained by the church shows the detail needed for later recording in the disbursement record.

The smaller church would probably use the conventional check stub form. As a church becomes larger and the check-writing task multiplies, the convenience and time-saving feature of the voucher check form might outweigh its added cost.

EXHIBIT 4-3
BLANK CHECK AND STUB

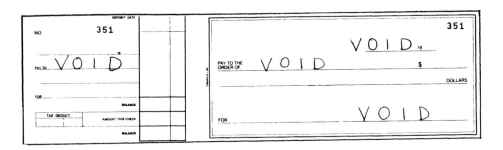

EXHIBIT 4-4
VOUCHER CHECK

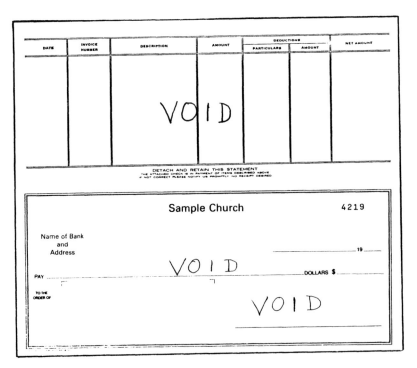

Chapter 5
Accounting Rules and Procedures

This chapter contains a brief description of the normal bookkeeping or accounting cycle. The following chapter will illustrate how to keep the books for a small to medium-sized church. Only when necessary is the language which is used that of the bookkeeper or accountant. The descriptions include only the very basic terms that are usually encountered. If the reader will take a few minutes to grasp the basic terms and rules, a sense of accomplishment and even excitement may be experienced. Much of the work of the bookkeeper or accountant is clerical in nature and quite detailed, but an understanding of basic concepts and definitions can indeed make it more interesting.

An entire accounting or bookkeeping cycle is one year in length and encompasses twelve one-month cycles that are simply repeated. The twelve-month period for accounting purposes, known as the *fiscal year* (see Glossary for definition of italicized terms), may coincide with the calendar year or end in any other month. The cycle begins with *transactions*, i.e., receipts and payments of cash, and ends with the preparation of reports for the church membership. Transactions are initially recorded in the *journal*, a book of original entry, and subsequently posted to *accounts* for the purpose of further summarizing the data by predetermined categories. The accounts comprise the *ledger* and should be the same as the accounts in the church approved budget. Transactions, both cash receipts and cash disbursements, are written in the journal, or journalized, in date order. As shown in later examples, other information also included in the journal is the amount, accounts involved, and any needed explanation.

Following is a summary of the sequence involved in the bookkeeping process:

Transactions, receipts and payments of cash,

$\downarrow$

are recorded in the journal,

$\downarrow$

and then posted to accounts in the ledger.

$\downarrow$

From the ledger, reports are prepared for the membership.

The Accounting Equation

As a basis for our discussion of the dual recording of transactions and the self-balancing nature of accounting records, a word of explanation of the *accounting equation* is in order. Stated simply, in algebraic form, the equation is as follows:

$$\text{Assets} = \text{Equity (of creditors and owners)}$$

Assets are generally defined as the resources owned by a business entity. For example, the assets of a retail department store consist of cash, the merchandise being held for sale, the store fixtures and equipment, and perhaps the building itself. Businesses operate for a profit and thus must reflect on their records all their assets and how they are used or consumed in the process of earning a profit. Churches do not operate for a profit, but they must also keep track of their assets. However, the only assets that we will account for or record in the accounting equation are cash and other such liquid assets. In fact, we can think of accounting for churches as keeping up with a cash fund. We are primarily concerned with the flow of cash and identifying the sources of that inflow—primarily member contributions—and the uses of the cash or outflow—to pay the operating expenses of the church. The above equation expresses the fact that the assets are contributed by creditors and owners, as is the case in most profit-oriented business enterprises. For our purposes, the equation can be reduced to the following terms:

$$\text{Assets (cash)} = \text{Fund balance}$$

Thus, in church accounting, as in other not-for-profit entities, we adopt the same basic accounting rules and framework used by business entities. There is no need to include liabilities (amounts owed to creditors) and owners' equity (represented in businesses by contributed capital or investment by owners). We are merely accounting for funds that are acquired by donation from members and keeping a record of how the funds are spent. Perhaps this is the reason accountants use the term *fund accounting* when referring to the unique sense in which accounting rules apply to not-for-profit entities such as churches and many governmental agencies.

To illustrate briefly the manner in which transactions are expressed in the equation, consider the following example. On January 1, 1980, XYZ Church had a checking account balance of $800 in their operating fund. In equation form this would appear as follows:

$$\frac{\text{Assets}}{\text{Cash balance } 800} = \frac{\text{Fund balance}}{800}$$

Assume that during the month of January total member contributions were $2,100 and total expenditures $2,050. These transactions would be expressed in the equation as follows:

	Assets	=	Fund balance
Cash balance, Jan. 1	+ 800		+ 800
Contributions	+2,100		+2,100
Expenditures	– 2,050		– 2,050
Cash balance, Jan. 31 =	+ 850		+ 850

At the end of January, XYZ had a cash balance of $850. This $50 increase in cash was due to an excess of member contributions over expenditures. In a later section we will examine how to record and keep up with the details surrounding each of the individual transactions that make up these totals. However, the end result will be the same as that expressed in the equation above. The equation is important because it forms the basis for double-entry bookkeeping. As you will see in a later section, it also forms the basis for organizing the accounts in the ledger. In the next few paragraphs we will consider the essential features of the journal and ledger accounts and their role in recording and summarizing transactions.

Recording Transactions in the Journal and Ledger

Almost all of the church's transactions will involve the receiving and paying of cash. Cash payments, for example, require checks to be written. A receipt of cash requires a bank deposit to be made. Both types of transactions are recorded initially on the checkbook stubs to preserve a record of payments and receipts and to keep a running balance of cash in the bank. This initial recording of trans-

actions, while necessary, does not provide needed summaries by account classifications. The *journal* and *ledger* make this task much easier. The journal is a device used for recording transactions in chronological sequence, showing the accounts debited and credited as well as amounts and providing space for an explanation if one is needed. The journal form shown here, the traditional two-column journal (often referred to as the general journal), is usually supplemented by one or more special journals, all serving the same essential function. Since most transactions in churches involve either the receipt or payment of cash, it would be possible to have a separate journal for cash receipts and also one for cash payments.

The journal form for smaller churches illustrated in chapter 6 combines transactions for receipts and payments (see Exhibit 6-1). Any journal entries that are necessary for other than cash transactions are recorded in the cash receipts and disbursements journal and appropriately identified. Transactions are entered from the report of deposit (illustrated in chapter 3) and the checkbook (described in chapter 4) directly into the cash receipts and disbursements journal. Both the date and check number are entered for payments. Checks as well as deposits are recorded in date order.

At the end of the month, after transactions have been recorded, or journalized, and totals obtained, the results must be posted to accounts in the ledger. Finally, from the ledger the statement of receipts and disbursements will be prepared.

The Journal

One of the first bookkeeping rules we must remember is that each transaction requires dual recording. In effect, two accounts will usually be involved: an account must be debited and a different account credited. Or if it is a complex transaction, it may have one or more debits and one or more credits. By following this rule, the bookkeeper is afforded a built-in check on accuracy because the accounts are self-balancing. Since equality is required, this rule is also consistent with the accounting equation.

The design of the traditional two-column journal, illustrated below, emphasizes the need for equality and provides this check. Observe that the journal has a column for the date, account and/or explanation, ledger reference, and debit and credit amounts.

Date	Account/Explanation	Ref.	Amount	
			Dr.	Cr.
XXX	Debit account 　　Credit account (Explanation, if needed, is entered in this space.)		XXX	XXX

The importance of the dual recording rule will be illustrated later in a sample problem.

The Ledger Account

There is a considerable period of history and tradition behind the ledger as we know it today. When bookkeeping rules were developed almost 500 years ago, the ledger account had a left side (the *debit* side, abbreviated dr.) and a right side (the *credit* side, abbreviated cr.). The form and content of the traditional account appears as follows:

(Debit)				(Credit)			
Date	Explanation	Ref.	Amount	Date	Explanation	Ref.	Amount

The next illustration shows that the account layout may be arranged differently, but regardless of its form, an account serves the purpose of tabulating additions and deductions. All accounts contain space for the same basic information including the date of the transaction, an explanation, a reference to the transaction data, and the amount. Perhaps the most convenient form of account contains a third column for recording the account balance, as illustrated below:

Date	Explanation	Ref.	Amount		
			Dr.	Cr.	Balance

The above account is easier to keep because it provides a space for recording the balance after each transaction. This form is used later in our illustrative problem.

At this point we have considered the two basic devices used by the accountant in recording and subsequently summarizing transactions—the journal and the ledger account—and also the rule that transactions require dual recording. Now a second rule is needed to define how a transaction involving the receipt of cash and the payment of cash may be expressed in debit and credit fashion. For example, in the cash account, *the receipt of cash is always recorded as a debit, and the payment of cash a credit.* Not only does this rule tell us how to record transactions, but it also dictates that the normal cash balance will be a debit. Thus, an excess of receipts over payments will leave an amount of cash on hand—a debit balance. It also follows that if a bank overdraft occurs, or the bank account is overspent, the balance would be a credit—one hopes this would be an infrequent occurrence. At any rate, if this rule is followed, cash and other similar asset accounts will normally have debit balances.

Having established these two basic rules, consider how the recording of a cash transaction in debits and credits is expressed. Assuming that cash is received from member contributions on Sunday, October 2, totaling $815, it would be recorded as a *debit* to the cash account. To make this entry balance and have debits equal credits, one or more accounts must be credited. In this case, the *credit* is to a single budget account—Receipts—Member Contributions. This entry, when recorded in two-column journal form, would appear as follows:

General Journal — Page 1

Date	Ref.	Account/Explanation	Ref.	Dr.	Cr.
1978 Oct.	2	Cash Receipts—member contributions (Explanation, if necessary)		815	815

In the above entry cash is increased by $815, a debit, and budget receipts are increased by a like amount.

Assume, next, a payment is made in cash to purchase literature and supplies on October 3, for a total cost of $135. This transaction would be recorded as a *credit* to cash and a *debit* to the budget account—literature, materials, and supplies—as follows:

General Journal — Page 1

Date	Ref.	Account/Explanation	Ref.	Dr.	Cr.
Oct.	3	Literature, Materials, and Supplies Cash (Explanation, if necessary)		135	135

Following are the ledger accounts involved in our example, given in summary or "T" account form, to illustrate how the journal entries are posted and thereby accumulated. The reader should observe the relationship between the different accounts.

Cash

(dr.)		(cr.)	
Balance, Oct. 1	1,150	Oct. 3, payment	135
Oct. 2, receipts	815		
Balance	1,830*		

*(1,150 + 815 - 135 = 1,830)

Budget Accounts

Receipts:

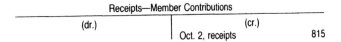

Expenditures:

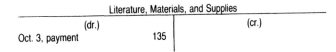

In the above illustration, the cash balance assumed to be on hand at the beginning of October, $1,150, is shown as a debit in the cash account. A cash overdraft, if it should occur, would appear as a credit. Observe also that the contributions' amount, $815, is posted to the budget account for receipts as a credit. The expenditure of cash for supplies, $135, is posted to the literature, materials, and supplies account as a debit. This relationship follows from the rule of dual recording and the further rule that a receipt of cash is recorded as a debit to the cash account and the payment of cash a credit to the cash account. The cash balance in the ledger account after posting the above transactions is $1,830 (1,150 + 815 − 135); the balance in the account for receipts from member contributions, $815; and the balance in the literature and supplies account, $135.

The Equation Restated

Returning to the accounting equation, we can now expand it to include all the details necessary for our purposes. In fact, in the example below, provision is made for inclusion of the entire set of accounts that will be used later in our illustrative problem. The accounts are presented in "T" account form, organized according to the budget categories presented in chapter 3. For the purpose of identification they are labeled Group I (operating fund accounts) and Group II (savings accounts).

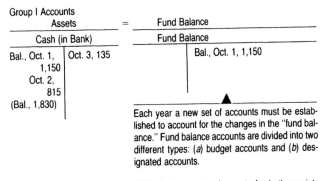

Each year a new set of accounts must be established to account for the changes in the "fund balance." Fund balance accounts are divided into two different types: (a) budget accounts and (b) designated accounts.

(a) Budget accounts. Accounts for both receipts and disbursements are necessary. Receipts are additions to the fund balance. Only one account is needed for recording receipts, as follows.

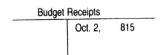

Cash disbursements, deductions from the fund balance, are recorded in accounts for budget items, as follows:

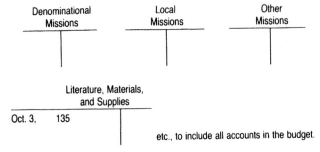

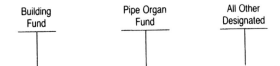

etc., to include all accounts in the budget.

(b) In addition, designated accounts such as the following are needed for transactions involving cash receipts and payments that are designated by donors for specific purposes:

Building Fund   Pipe Organ Fund   All Other Designated

Throughout our examples, cash that is donated for the building and pipe organ funds, as well as excess cash for operating needs, is kept in a savings account. The above accounts will reflect a cash receipt and also a cash payment when this is the case. The fund transfer reduces assets in the operating fund and increases assets in the savings (or restricted) fund, shown below as Group II.

The above accounts also illustrate the self-balancing feature of the equation. Initially the cash-in-bank account, a debit of $1,150, is equal to the fund balance account, a credit of $1,150. Thus, the equation is in balance at the beginning of the period. You should also note that the equation balances after the above transactions have been posted, determined as follows:

Cash, ending balance (dr.) 1,830 = Fund balance, beginning (cr.)   1,150
                                         Add: Receipts (cr.)   + 815
                                         Less: Disbursements (dr.)   − 135
                                         Equals ending balance (cr.)   1,830

As stated above, cash in excess of current operating needs as well as cash being accumulated for the building or a pipe organ is kept in a savings account. Likewise, this account is a separate fund. As such it would have its own set of self-balancing accounts similar to the checking account above. In abbreviated form the accounts for this fund are as follows:

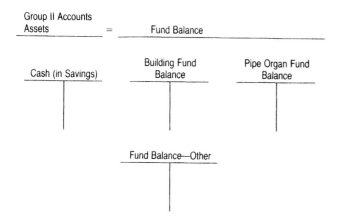

Perhaps with this overall picture in mind, you will be able to comprehend better the description of the ledger accounts for Sample Church in chapter 6.

Chapter 6
The Accounting Process Illustrated

Sample Church has been in existence several years, organized as a mission in a newly developing community. It was initially sponsored and partially supported by a neighboring church. Sample Church is now self-supporting and is debt-free except for a loan obtained from a local bank to purchase an adjacent lot for parking and for future expansion. Church membership is made up of approximately eighty families. Regular services are held on Sunday mornings and evenings as well as Wednesday evenings. Sunday morning Bible study classes are held preceding the congregational worship service. Sunday evening services consist of small group study sessions followed by a short worship service. On Wednesdays a buffet-style meal is served. The church staff consists of a full-time pastor, a full-time church secretary, and a part-time music director as available.

In addition to typing correspondence and other duties, the secretary writes all checks. She also makes the entries to record the checks and deposits in the cash receipts and disbursements journal. Each month the treasurer totals and balances the journal and prepares the financial statements. The monthly bank reconciliation is prepared by the treasurer and periodically is reviewed by the chairman of the finance committee. The finance committee, comprised of three members, is responsible for compiling the annual budget. The finance committee chairman signs all checks and assists the treasurer as necessary in implementing the budget.

Chapter 6 follows transactions for the month of December to show how they are recorded in the journal and posted to the ledger accounts of Sample Church. Chapter 7 will describe the completion of the reporting cycle, showing how statements are prepared from the ledger accounts.

The Combined Cash Receipts and Disbursements Journal

Exhibit 6-1 shows the cash receipts and disbursements of Sample Church for the month of December. Both the account numbers and the names of the debit and credit components are given across the top of the pages. The account numbers are the same as those presented earlier in the budget for Sample Church (Exhibit 2-1). Since most of the transactions involve making deposits in the checking account and writing checks thereon, the first two columns

are used for this purpose. The first column, cash receipts, is a debit, and the second column, cash payments, is a credit. The remaining columns are assigned to the most active accounts to simplify later postings from the journal to ledger accounts. Columns 3 through 8 are assigned to the following accounts in the order listed: literature and training materials, music and choirs, office supplies and bulletins, utilities, kitchen, and salaries and allowances. The next two columns, 9 and 10, are for F.I.C.A. taxes and income taxes. Column 11 is for budget receipts, and 12 and 13 are used for all other accounts. Space is provided in columns 14 through 16 to write the account number and account title for the amounts recorded in columns 12 and 13.

Each column is appropriately labeled in debit and credit fashion. With the exception of cash, which has separate columns for debits and credits, and payroll taxes that utilize two columns, accounts have only a single column for recording amounts. However, it is desirable in some cases to enter a credit amount in a debit column. If this is done, the credit should be either written in red or entered in parentheses ( ) to avoid errors later when the journal is totaled. This procedure is illustrated in columns 7, 9, and 10. The kitchen account, column 7, is debited for food purchases along with other expenditures and is credited for cash receipts from member payments for meals. Columns 9 and 10 are necessary for recording the withholding of payroll taxes and subsequent payment of these taxes to the appropriate federal and state agencies. In column 9, F.I.C.A. taxes are entered first as a credit when deducted from the employee and secondly as a debit when paid to the bank or designated depository. Likewise, in column 10, income taxes withheld are entered as a credit and subsequently as a debit.

As explained in chapter 7 (under "Payroll Tax Filing and Reporting"), and assuming the church has elected to be covered by Social Security, churches are required to match amounts withheld from employees. Taxes that were formerly called F.I.C.A. taxes are now separated into Social Security (in 1996, 6.2 percent on the first $62,700) and Medicare (in 1996, 1.45 percent on all wages paid). While the new rates and terminology are not reflected in the illustrations, the amount withheld for each tax would

EXHIBIT 6-1
CASH RECEIPTS AND DISBURSEMENTS JOURNAL

			1	2	3	4	5	6	7
			101		401	404	601	603	606
		Ck. No.	Cash	Cash	Literature + training materials	Music + choirs	Office supplies + bulletins	Utilities	Kitchen
Date	Payee/Description		Receipts Dr.	Payments Cr.	Dr.	Dr.	Dr.	Dr.	Dr. (Cr.)
1	City Bank	101		127.00					
6	Greene Flower	102		18.00					
12	Piano Tuner	103		29.00		29.00			
15	Paul Able	104		588.00					
15	Mary James	105		237.00					
15	Best Foods, Inc.	106		156.00					156.00
16	Christian Book Store	107		16.00					
16	Postmaster	108		65.00					
20	Mary James	109		44.00	19.00				14.00
20	Abbott Pest Control	110		28.00					
24	Local Power + Lt.	111		87.00				87.00	
24	Natural Gas Co.	112		54.00				54.00	
24	Cooke Tel. Co.	113		68.00					
26	Typewriter Co., Inc.	114		27.00					
26	Literature Supply Co.	115		35.00	35.00				
28	Paul Able	116		588.00					
28	Mary James	117		237.00					
30	State Convention	118		1002.00					
30	State Revenue Serv.	119		126.00					
30	City Bank	170		394.00					
31	Blue Cross Inc.	171		47.00					
31	Bank charge	—		4.00			4.00		
31	Local Power + Lt.	172		65.00					
31	First Savings Assn.	173		200.00					
31	Journal entry to savings account								
26									
31	Children's Home	174		56.00					
28									
29									
31	Deposit		1475.00						(101.00
9	Deposit		1114.00						(87.00
16	Deposit		1477.00						(76.00
23	Deposit		1330.00						(101.00
30	Deposit		2082.00					(10.00)	(80.00
35									
36									
37			7478.00	4289.00	54.00	29.00	4.00	133.00	Dr. 170.00
38									(Cr. 445.00
39									
40									
41									
42									

	Salaries + allowances Dr. (501,503)	F.I.C.A. taxes Dr. (Cr.) (610)	Income taxes withheld Dr. (Cr) (201)	Budget receipts Cr.	Other Accounts — Amount Dr.	Or.	Account number	Account/Explanation	
					127⁰⁰		801	debt retirement	1
					18⁰⁰		612	flowers	2
									3
501	625⁰⁰		{ 121⁰⁰ 16⁰⁰		100 00		607	car allowance + mileage	4
503	300⁰⁰	(18⁰⁰)	{ 40⁰⁰ 3⁰⁰ }						5
									6
					12⁰⁰		406	library	7
					65⁰⁰		607	postage	8
					11⁰⁰		607	car allowance + mileage	9
					28⁰⁰		701	maintenance - bldg. repair	10
									11
									12
					68⁰⁰		604	telephone	13
					22⁰⁰		702	maintenance - office	14
									15
501	625⁰⁰		{ 121⁰⁰ 16⁰⁰		100⁰⁰		607	car allowance + mileage	16
503	300⁰⁰	(18⁰⁰)	{ 40⁰⁰ 3⁰⁰ }						17
					100⁷⁰⁰		301	missions - denominational	18
			124⁰⁰						19
		72⁰⁰	322⁰⁰						20
					47⁰⁰		604	hospital insurance	21
									22
					65⁰⁰		903	designated - other	23
					200⁰⁰		901	designated - bldg. fund	24
					200⁰⁰		151	cash in savings acct	25
						200⁰⁰	161	building fund balance	26
					50⁰⁰		903	designated - other	27
									28
									29
				1324⁰⁰		50⁰⁰	903	designated - other	30
				1017⁰⁰		10⁰⁰	406	library	31
				1381⁰⁰					32
				1164⁰⁰		65⁰⁰	903	designated - other	33
				1797⁰⁰		200⁰⁰	901	designated - bldg. fund	34
									35
									36
501	1250⁰⁰		448⁰⁰	6678⁰⁰	2119⁰⁰	525⁰⁰	—		37
503	600⁰⁰	(36⁰⁰)	(364⁰⁰)		241⁰⁰		607	Recap- car allowances	38
									39
									40
									41
									42

be entered in the F.I.C.A. column as a credit. Thus, the net effect of payroll taxes in account 610 is a debit, or a budget expenditure, equal to the church's matching portion of Social Security and Medicare taxes.

A further explanation of the journal is presented in the following pages by giving specific transactions and how they are recorded.

Disbursements

Perhaps you will want to look over the entire list of transactions first. Next review the manner in which each transaction is entered in the journal. By carefully observing the procedures that are illustrated for recording the illustrative transactions, you will be better able to determine how similar but unlike transactions are to be recorded.

Date	Transaction and Explanation	Check Number	Amount
Dec. 1	Monthly payment to City Bank for principal and interest on note: $106 and $21, respectively.	101	$127
	Credit: 101 Cash		
	Debit: 801 Note payment		
6	Green's Flowers: invoice dated Nov. 30, flower arrangement for church services.	102	18
	Credit: 101 Cash		
	Debit: 612 Flowers		
12	Piano Tuners: for services in tuning piano.	103	29
	Credit: 101 Cash		
	Debit: 404 Music & choirs		
15	Paul Able, pastor: salary and allowances for Dec. 1-15, net of withholdings as follows: gross salary, $525; federal income tax withheld, $121; state income tax withheld, $16; equals net pay, $388. The housing allowance of $100 per month is added to the gross salary, giving a total of $625 in account 501. The car allowance, $100 per month, is added to the net pay and housing allowance, giving total pay of $588 (388 + 100 + 100). As explained in chapter 5, the allowance for car and housing normally are not subject to income tax.	104	588
	Credit: 101 Cash	$588	
	Credit: 610 Federal income taxes withheld	121	
	Credit: 610 State income taxes withheld	16	

	Debit: 501 Salaries and allowances (salary plus housing allowance)	625	
	Debit: 607 Car allowance and mileage	100	
15	Mary James, secretary: salary for Dec. 1-15, as follows: gross earnings, $300; federal income tax withheld, $40; state income tax withheld, $5; F.I.C.A. taxes withheld, $18; net pay, $237.	105	237
	Credit: 101 Cash	$237	
	Credit: 610 Federal income tax withheld	40	
	Credit: 610 State income tax withheld	5	
	Credit: 610 F.I.C.A. tax withheld	18	
	Debit: 503 Salary, secretary	300	
15	Best Foods, Inc.: for meats, produce, and canned foods for kitchen.	106	156
	Credit: 101 Cash		
	Debit: 606 Kitchen		
16	Christian Book Store: for library books.	107	16
	Credit: 101 Cash		
	Debit: 406 Library		
16	Postmaster: for postage stamps.	108	65
	Credit: 101 Cash		
	Debit: 602 Postage		
20	Mary James, petty cash custodian: To reimburse petty cash fund for amounts spent, as follows: Sunday school materials, $19; parking and transportation, $11; grocery tickets for kitchen supplies, $14; total, $44. (A $50 cash fund is kept by Mary James for making minor purchases. It is reimbursed periodically for the amount spent to maintain a $50 balance.)	109	44
	Credit: 101 Cash	$44	
	Debit: 401 Literature and materials	19	
	Debit: 606 Kitchen	14	
	Debit: 607 Car allowance and mileage	11	
22	Abbott Pest Control: for quarterly services.	110	28
	Credit: 101 Cash		
	Debit: 701 Maintenance		
24	Local Power & Light Co.: electric bill for period Nov. 15 to Dec. 15.	111	89

Credit: 101 Cash
Debit: 603 Utilities

24	Natural Gas Co.: gas for heating for period Nov. 17 to Dec. 17. Credit: 101 Cash Debit: 603 Utilities	112	54
26	Cooke Telephone Company: local and long distance calls for month ended Dec. 21. Credit: 101 Cash Debit: 604 Telephone	113	68
26	Typewriter Service, Inc.: for typewriter repairs. Credit: 101 Cash Debit: 702 Maintenance	114	22
26	Literature Supply Co.: quarterly supplies for Sunday Bible classes. Credit: 101 Cash Debit: 401 Literature and materials	115	35
28	Paul Able, pastor: salary & allowances, Dec. 15-31 For explanation, refer to check no. 104 above.	116	588
28	Mary James, secretary: salary, Dec. 15-31. For explanation, refer to check no. 105 above.	117	237
31	State Convention Board: payment for denominational missions as follows: 15 percent of Dec. undesignated receipts, or $1,002. Credit: 101 Cash Debit: 301 Denominational missions	118	1,002
31	State Revenue Service: for quarterly taxes withheld. Credit: 101 Cash Debit: 610 State income taxes withheld	119	126
31	City Bank: for deposit of Dec. payroll taxes as follows: Federal taxes withheld, $322; F.I.C.A. taxes withheld, $36; plus F.I.C.A. taxes paid by employer, $36. Credit: 101 Cash $394 Debit: 610 Federal income taxes withheld 322 Debit: 610 F.I.C.A. taxes withheld 36	120	394

	Debit: 610 F.I.C.A. taxes, employer 36		
31	Blue Cross Insurance Co.: for hospital insurance, on employees, month of December. Credit: 101 Cash Debit: 609 Employee's insurance	121	47
31	A bank service charge of $4 appeared on the December bank statement. Credit: 101 Cash Debit: 601 Office supplies and expenses	—	4
31	Local Power & Light: payment of a gift designated for needy family's light bill. Credit: 101 Cash Debit: 903 Designated (benevolence)	122	65
31	First Savings Assn.: deposit in savings of a designated gift to the building fund. (The deposit was entered in cash receipts on Dec. 30—see Exhibit 3-4.) Credit: 101 Cash Debit: 901 Designated—bldg. fund Immediately following this entry, record the following journal entry, in columns 12-16, to reflect the addition of cash to the separate fund for savings and to its fund balance: Credit: 161 Building fund balance: $200 Debit: 151 Cash—savings account: $200	123	200
31	Children's Home: payment of a designated gift received December 2. Credit: 101 Cash Debit: 903 Designated	124	50

You should take ample time to study the layout of the journal and see how each of the transactions has been journalized. While you may not be able to use the exact columnar headings in setting up a journal for your church, you should try to set up columns that seem to fit best your budget categories and accounts.

The above list of disbursements contains the checks written during December and also several written after the end of the month in early January. The reason for entering these January checks in December is to present more accurately the financial activities involved in a particular month. Check

118, for example, is for payment of the state mission offering, computed as 15 percent of receipts for December. This check would normally be written in early January after book receipts for December were verified with the bank reconciliation. By the secretary's entering the check in December, the payment is shown in the same month as the offering receipts. Payroll taxes are treated in a similar manner. Checks 119 and 120 in payment of December taxes would normally be prepared early in January after the December disbursements for payroll had been made. Also, the payment of most designated offerings as well as fund transfers are usually made at the end of the month or shortly thereafter. For example, checks 122 and 124 are in payment of designated gifts received in December. Likewise, check 123 written in January is for transfer of a designated gift in December from the checking account to the savings account. To aid the bookkeeper in entering these disbursements each month, a checklist such as the one below should be prepared.

1. After all payroll checks have been written for the month, determine F.I.C.A. taxes and federal withholding taxes and write a check for the amount of the deposit. In many cases the actual deposit does not need to be given to the bank or other depository until the fifteenth of the following month. While the check will be entered in the current month, it will not be necessary to release or deliver it until the due date.

2. Determine the amount of state income taxes that have been withheld, payable each quarter, in our example, and enter the check in the last month of the quarter. (Since we paid state income taxes only once during the quarter, the result is not entirely consistent with the handling of federal taxes that are deposited monthly. Taxes withheld in December were $42 and those paid in December, $126, or an $84 excess of payment over withholding. However, the amounts involved are considerably smaller and result in only a slight distortion in any single month.) To determine the requirements in your state, contact your department of revenue.

3. Prepare checks for any designated amounts received in the current month unless the donor has given instructions to the contrary. In some cases payment must be withheld temporarily to determine the intent of the donor. Also, prepare checks for amounts payable to mission causes, for scholarships, as well as organ and building fund contributions. (As an alternative procedure, some churches do not run all their deposits for building fund, organ fund, debt retirement, etc., through the operating fund checking account, but rather make the deposit initially into a savings account or even a separate checking account. The procedure adopted by a given church will probably depend on the nature as well as the timing of receipts. For example, if the donor gives a single check and specifies that part of it goes to the operating fund, part to the building fund, and part to the organ fund or other designated causes, perhaps the best procedure is the one illustrated above—to deposit the check initially in the operating fund checking account and subsequently transfer it to the other designated causes.)

4. Interest earned on savings deposits should be recorded on the books at least once each year. To record the interest, the savings account should be increased by a debit, and the interest earned added to the fund balance by a credit.

Receipts

In December, five bank deposits were made, one for each Sunday of the month. The information below is a summary of the weekly deposit reports prepared by the counters. Details of the December 30 deposit are presented in Exhibit 3-4 in chapter 3 on cash receipts. Observe in the journal (see Exhibit 6-1) how each deposit total is recorded as a debit to cash with credits to one or more accounts that equal this total.

Date		Amount
Dec. 2	Weekly deposit of Sunday offerings, a total of $1,475. Included is an offering designated for the State Children's Home, $50, and kitchen receipts, $101.	$1,475
	Debit: 101 Cash $1,475	
	Credit: 201 Receipts— undesignated 1,324	
	903 Receipts— designated 50	
	606 Kitchen 101	
Dec. 9	Weekly deposit of Sunday offerings, $1,114, including $87 in kitchen receipts and $10 for library.	1,114
	Debit: 101 Cash $1,114	
	Credit: 201 Receipts— undesignated 1,017	
	406 Library 10	
	606 Kitchen 87	
Dec. 16	Weekly deposit of Sunday offerings, $1,477, including $96 in kitchen receipts.	1,477
	Debit: 101 Cash $1,477	
	Credit: 201 Receipts— undesignated 1,381	
	606 Kitchen 96	
Dec. 23	Weekly deposit of Sunday offering, $1,330, including $101 in kitchen receipts and $65 for a local benevolence.	1,330
	Debit: 101 Cash $1,330	
	Credit: 201 Receipts— undesignated 1,164	
	903 Receipts— designated 65	
	606 Kitchen 101	

Dec. 30   Weekly deposit of Sunday offering,   2,082
           $2,082, including $80 in kitchen re-
           ceipts, $10 fee for use of church by
           nonmembers for a wedding, and a
           $200 building fund contribution.

Debit: 101 Cash	$2,082	
Credit: 201 Receipts—		
undesignated	1,792	
603 Receipts—		
designated	10	
606 Kitchen	80	
901 Receipts		
designated	200	

Again, the reader should review carefully each deposit and how it is recorded. In the paragraphs below several comments are offered to explain the unusual items.

The December 2 deposit includes a $50 gift from a member designated specifically for the Children's Home. Payment of this amount is made on December 31, check 124. Gifts for designated causes should be paid promptly and in keeping with the donor's request. Also on December 2, receipts of $101 are deposited from the Wednesday supper. This amount is recorded as a credit to the kitchen account, number 606. Since the kitchen account is debited for food purchases and credited for receipts applicable to meals, the account balance will produce a "net" result, reflecting both debits and credits. When preparing the report for the membership, some churches want to know both the receipts and expenditures applicable to such accounts. In such cases, totals for each should be presented instead of showing only the net amount.

The deposit for December 9 includes a $10 gift to be used for library subscriptions and books. Similar to the entry for kitchen receipts, this amount is recorded as a credit to the library account. When the funds are spent, a charge will be made to the library account also giving a net effect.

On December 23, a gift of $65 was received from a member to be used for local benevolence purposes. It was decided by the benevolence committee to apply this amount toward the electric power bill of a local family in severe financial need.

On December 30, two unusual items are noted. A nonmember was charged a $10 fee for use of the church for a wedding. This fee is charged to help defray the added cost involved in heating and lighting and is credited to the utility account. Also, a $200 donation was received for the building fund. Such amounts are usually deposited in the checking account and transferred each month to a savings account. In addition to the entry to record the payment of this designated gift from checking to savings, check 123 on December 31, a journal entry is made to record a debit to the savings account and a credit to the building fund balance. This entry is made in the journal immediately following the check recording the transfer. An explanation of the debit and credit entries was given above with check 123 in the section on disbursement.

Prove Accuracy of Cash Receipts and Disbursements Journal

After all entries have been recorded, each column is added and totals entered in pencil or pen as illustrated. Column 7, the kitchen account, contains both debit and credit entries. Separate totals are entered in this case. This is also true of columns 9 and 10, both of which have debit and credit entries. Column 8 reflects transactions for accounts 501 and 503, salaries and allowances. Each account total is computed and entered in pencil to enable separate posting. Since columns 12 and 13 contain a mixture of different accounts, these column totals will not be posted. They will be used only to balance the journal. As explained in a later section, postings from the "other" columns are made easier when amounts to be posted to the same account are combined, resulting in a single posting to each account involved.

When all columns have been added, the final step is to prove that total debits equal total credits. While this step may be done on the adding machine, the following tabulation is presented for illustration purposes.

Column totals—cash receipts and disbursements journal

Account No.	Debits	Account No.	Credits
101	7,478	101	4,289
401	54	606	465
404	29	610	36
601	4	610	364
603	133	201	6,678
606	170	Other	525
501	1,250		
503	600		
610	72		
610	448		
Other	2,119		
Totals	12,357		12,357

The Ledger

After transactions for December have been recorded in the journal and the journal is in balance, the next step is to post the amounts to the ledger where they are combined with prior months' data. Postings for the current month are added to the amounts for prior months to obtain year-to-date totals. However, before we look at the actual ledger accounts and postings for Sample Church, let us review briefly the structure of the ledger and the relationship between the accounts discussed earlier.

Structure of the Ledger for Sample Church

The ledger contains two self-balancing groups of accounts, identified earlier, as follows:

Group I
  Operating fund accounts—for checking account transactions, including:
  (*a*) Budget accounts for unrestricted (undesignated) receipts and budget expenditures and
  (*b*) Accounts for restricted (designated) receipts and expenditures

Group II
  Funds in savings—restricted and unrestricted

As already stated in this chapter, most churches receive gifts that are designated or restricted for a specified purpose. Examples are gifts for building fund, organ fund, special benevolence offerings for persons in financial need, or offerings for home or foreign missions. Since most offerings of this nature are included with the members' regular offerings each week or month, the procedure recommended above was to deposit all such offerings in the regular (operating fund) checking account. Subsequently, they will be paid out of the checking account for the purpose specified by the donor. Group I (*b*) accounts are set up for transactions of this nature. All other receipts intended for the operating budget, those that are undesignated, along with the budget disbursements flow through Group I (*a*) accounts.

Group II accounts are for funds held in investments and savings. For bookkeeping purposes, a separate set of self-balancing accounts, or fund, is established. Thus, Group I and Group II are separate funds. The following diagram shows in condensed form the relationship within Group I accounts for Sample Church.

GROUP I OPERATING FUND ACCOUNTS

Cash in Checking   101

Date		Dr.	Cr.	Bal.
1979 Jan. 1	Balance			1,401

=

Operating Fund Balance   111

Date		Dr.	Cr.	Bal.
1979 Jan. 1	Balance			(1,401)

(*a*) Budget Accounts

Budget Receipts   201

	Dr.	Cr.	Bal.

Denominational Missions   301

	Dr.	Cr.	Bal.

etc., to include all accounts in the budget (see the chart of accounts earlier in chapter 4)

(*b*) Accounts for Designated Items

Building Fund   901

	Dr.	Cr.	Bal.

Pipe Organ Fund   902

	Dr.	Cr.	Bal.

All Other Designated Funds   903

	Dr.	Cr.	Bal.

Additional accounts may be added as necessary for specific items that need to be kept separate.

To review briefly, in the operating fund the relationship between the cash in checking (101) and operating fund balance (111) is that of an equation and can be expressed by an equal (=) sign. To complete the self-balancing feature inherent in the accounting framework, cash and any other such asset accounts are assigned debit balances. The fund balance and any other equity accounts are assigned credit balances. Thus, the asset side of the equation equals the equity or fund balance side. More importantly, debit totals are equal to credit totals, providing a check on clerical accuracy. At the beginning of the year, for Sample Church, the following equation expresses the balances that existed:

Cash, $1,401 dr. = Fund Balance, $1,401 cr.

These amounts are shown in the accounts above, with the credit balance shown in parentheses.

Budget accounts, Group I (*a*), are established each year to accumulate and classify cash inflows and outflows for budget items. The primary source of inflows is budget receipts (201) that are accumulated as credits. Outflows are for budget disbursements, beginning with account 301, and are accumulated as debits.

Accounts for designated items, Group I (*b*), are established each year to accumulate and classify designated cash inflows and the subsequent disposition of these inflows. These amounts will normally be received and disbursed within the same month. Thus, when the designated gifts are paid in the same month that they are received, the accounts will have zero balances. If for some reason there is a delay in making payment until the next month or even the next year, the payment will not be in the same period as the receipt. In case this happens, it is best simply to report the payment in the period it is actually made.

The diagram below shows the relationship within Group II accounts for Sample Church.

GROUP II FUNDS IN SAVINGS

Cash in Savings   151   =   Fund balance, or equity accounts, represented by:

Date		Dr.	Cr.	Bal.
1979 Jan. 1	Balance			16,834

Building Fund Balance—Restricted   161

Date		Dr.	Cr.	Bal.
1979 Jan. 1	Balance			(9,842)

Pipe Organ Fund Balance—Restricted   162

Date		Dr.	Cr.	Bal.
1979 Jan. 1	Balance			(5,201)

Fund Balance in Savings—Unrestricted   170

Date		Dr.	Cr.	Bal.
1979 Jan. 1	Balance			(1,791)

Additional accounts may be added as necessary if other funds are established.

The above relationship between the cash in savings (151) and the respective fund balances (161, 162, and 170) is that of an equation and is expressed by an equal (=) sign. Cash in savings and other such asset accounts have debit balances. On the other hand, fund balance accounts have credit balances. At the beginning of the year, for Sample Church, the following equation expresses the balances that existed:

Cash in savings, $16,834 = Building Fund Balance, $ 9,842

Pipe Organ Fund
Balance, 5,201

Fund Balance—
Unrestricted 1,791

Totals $16,834 $16,834

These amounts are shown in the accounts above as they appear in the ledger. Observe that credit balances are shown in parentheses. Throughout the year these accounts are used to record transfers to and from savings. Normally, gifts intended for these funds are first deposited with the undesignated gifts in the checking account. The offsetting credit is to one or more of the designated accounts included above in the Group 1 (*b*) category. Subsequently the gifts are transferred, preferably within the same month, from checking to savings. Funds will be held in savings to earn interest until they are needed for their intended purpose. At that time, the savings account and the fund balance will be reduced for the amount withdrawn. If payment is to be made by check, normally the funds will be redeposited in the checking account.

Ledger Accounts for Sample Church

Reproduced on the following pages is the complete ledger (Exhibit 6-2) for Sample Church. You should observe that the accounts show only the information for prior months that is needed for our purposes. In most cases, the accounts contain the November transactions and balances or simply the latest posting if there were no transactions in November. Accounts for checking and savings and their related fund balances (account numbers 101 and 111 for checking and 151, 161, 162, and 170 for savings) contain the beginning of year balances. These balances are necessary in completing the problem and also for preparing the financial reports illustrated in chapter 7.

**EXHIBIT 6-2
LEDGER ACCOUNTS
SAMPLE CHURCH**

I. Operating Fund

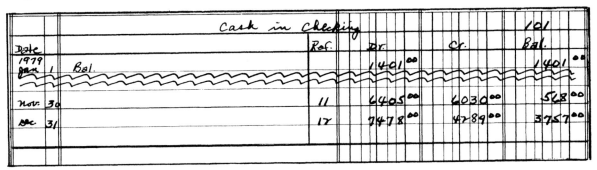

II. Funds in Savings—Restricted and Unrestricted

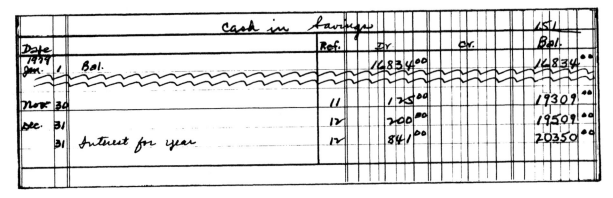

I. Operating Fund

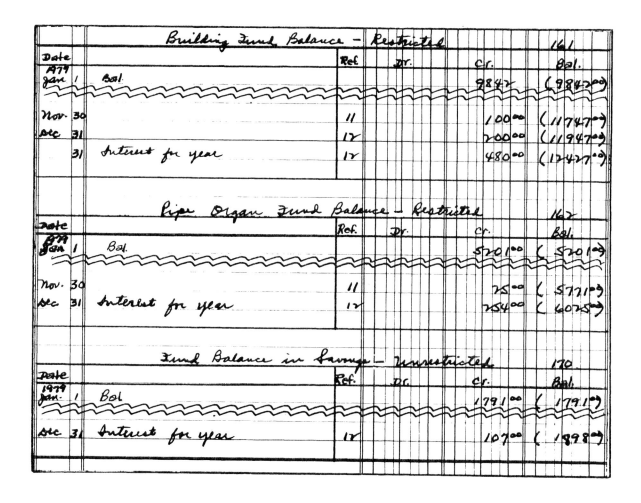

II. Funds in Savings—Restricted and Unrestricted

		Operating Fund Balance				111
Date			Ref.	Dr.	Cr.	Bal.
1979 Jan.	1	Bal.			1401 00	(1401 00)
Dec.	31	To close Group I(a) and I(b) accounts			2356 00	3757 00

		Building Fund Balance — Restricted				161
Date			Ref.	Dr.	Cr.	Bal.
1979 Jan.	1	Bal.			9842 00	(9842 00)
Nov.	30		11		100 00	(11747 00)
Dec.	31		12		200 00	(11947 00)
	31	Interest for year	12		480 00	(12427 00)

		Pipe Organ Fund Balance — Restricted				162
Date			Ref.	Dr.	Cr.	Bal.
1979 Jan.	1	Bal.			5701 00	(5701 00)
Nov.	30		11		75 00	(5771 00)
Dec.	31	Interest for year	12		254 00	(6025 00)

		Fund Balance in Savings — Unrestricted				170
Date			Ref.	Dr.	Cr.	Bal.
1979 Jan.	1	Bal			1791 00	(1791 00)
Dec.	31	Interest for year	12		107 00	(1898 00)

43

I (a) Operating Fund—Budget Accounts

Budget Receipts					**101**
Date		Ref.	Dr.	Cr.	Bal.
Nov. 30		11		3504 00	(54438 00)
Dec. 31		12		6678 00	(61116 00)

Denominational Missions					**301**
Date		Ref.	Dr.	Cr.	Bal.
Nov. 30		11	576 00		8165 00
Dec. 31		12	1002 00		9167 00

Local Missions					**302**
Date		Ref.	Dr.	Cr.	Bal.
Oct. 31		10	25 00		394 00

Other Missions					**303**
Date		Ref.	Dr.	Cr.	Bal.
Oct. 31		10	16 00		310 00

Literature and Training Materials					**401**
Date		Ref.	Dr.	Cr.	Bal.
Nov. 30		11	370 00		1541 00
Dec. 31		12	54 00		1595 00

Women's Missions and Auxiliaries					**402**
Date		Ref.	Dr.	Cr.	Bal.
Nov. 30		11	200 00		600 00

I (a)   Operating Fund—Budget Accounts   (continued)

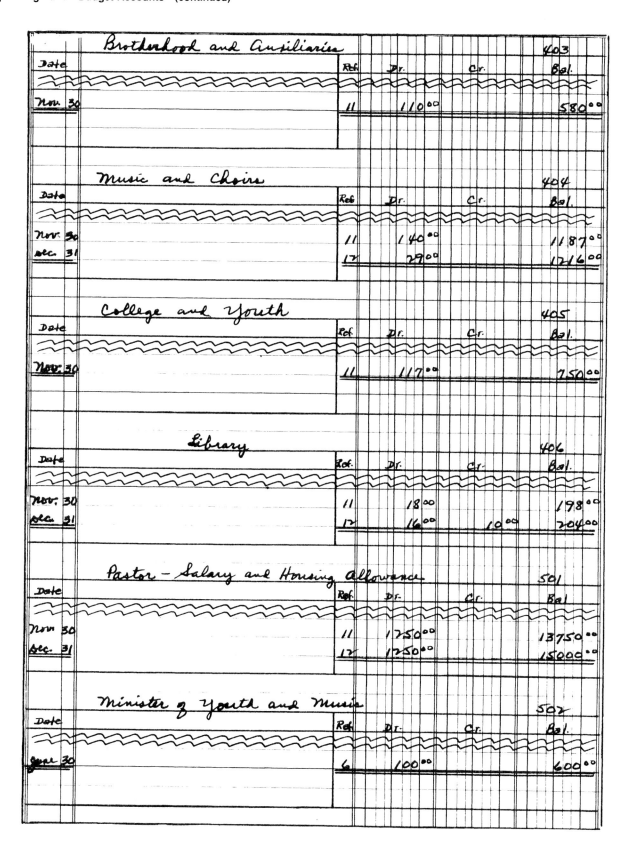

Brotherhood and Auxiliaries   403

Date		Ref.	Dr.	Cr.	Bal.
Nov. 30		11	110 00		580 00

Music and Choirs   404

Date		Ref.	Dr.	Cr.	Bal.
Nov. 30		11	140 00		1187 00
Dec. 31		12	29 00		1216 00

College and Youth   405

Date		Ref.	Dr.	Cr.	Bal.
Nov. 30		11	117 00		750 00

Library   406

Date		Ref.	Dr.	Cr.	Bal.
Nov. 30		11	18 00		198 00
Dec. 31		12	16 00	10 00	204 00

Pastor – Salary and Housing Allowance   501

Date		Ref.	Dr.	Cr.	Bal.
Nov. 30		11	1750 00		13750 00
Dec. 31		12	1250 00		15000 00

Minister of Youth and Music   502

Date		Ref.	Dr.	Cr.	Bal.
June 30		6	100 00		600 00

I (a) Operating Fund—Budget Accounts (continued)

Church Secretary — 503

Date		Ref.	Dr.	Cr.	Bal.
Nov. 30		11	600 00		6600 00
Dec. 31		17	600 00		7200 00

Janitorial — 504

Date		Ref.	Dr.	Cr.	Bal.
Nov. 30		11	150 00		1350 00

Part-time Help — 505

Date		Ref.	Dr.	Cr.	Bal.
Nov. 30		11	40 00		180 00

Office Supplies and Bulletins — 601

Date		Ref.	Dr.	Cr.	Bal.
Nov. 30		11	243 00		1901 00
Dec. 31		17	4 00		1905 00

Postage — 602

Date		Ref.	Dr.	Cr.	Bal.
Nov. 30		11	72 00		755 00
Dec. 31		17	65 00		820 00

Utilities — 603

Date		Ref.	Dr.	Cr.	Bal.
Nov. 30		11	140 00		3378 00
Dec. 31		17	133 00		3511 00

I (*a*)   Operating Fund—Budget Accounts   (continued)

Telephone   604

Date		Ref.	Dr.	Cr.	Bal.
Nov. 30		11	71 00		588 00
Dec. 31		12	68 00		656 00

Property Insurance   605

Date		Ref.	Dr.	Cr.	Bal.
Nov. 30		11	120		645 00

Kitchen   606

Date		Ref.	Dr.	Cr.	Bal.
Nov. 30		11	640 00	420 00	1152 00
Dec. 31		12	170 00	465 00	857 00

Car Allowance and Mileage   607

Date		Ref.	Dr.	Cr.	Bal.
Nov. 30		11	209 00		2378 00
Dec. 31		12	211 00		2589 00

Conventions and Conferences   608

Date		Ref.	Dr.	Cr.	Bal.
Nov. 30		11	62 00		480 00

Hospital Insurance and Retirement   609

Date		Ref.	Dr.	Cr.	Bal.
Nov. 30		11	164 00		1392 00
Dec. 31		12	47 00		1439 00

I (a)   Operating Fund—Budget Accounts   (continued)

F. I. C. A. Tax Expense — 610

Date			Ref.	Dr.	Cr.	Bal.
Nov. 30			11	72 00	36 00	
			11	322 00	322 00	234 00
Dec. 31			12	72 00	36 00	
			12	448 00	364 00	354 00

Publicity, Advertising, and Promotion — 611

Date			Ref.	Dr.	Cr.	Bal.
Nov. 30			11	41 00		352 00

Flowers, Decorations — 612

Date			Ref.	Dr.	Cr.	Bal.
Nov. 30			11	24 00		278 00
Dec. 31			12	18 00		296 00

Other — contingency — 613

Date			Ref.	Dr.	Cr.	Bal.
Nov. 30			11	82 00		730 00

Maintenance — Buildings and Grounds — 701

Date			Ref.	Dr.	Cr.	Bal.
Nov. 30			11	363 00		877 00
Dec. 31			12	28 00		905 00

Maintenance — Office and Other — 702

Date			Ref.	Dr.	Cr.	Bal.
Nov. 30			11	167 00		1260 00
Dec. 31			12	22 00		1282 00

I (a) Operating Fund—Budget Accounts (continued)

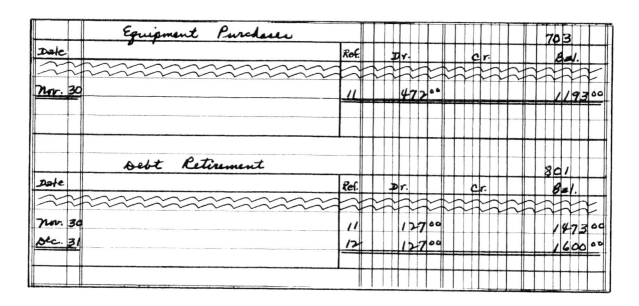

Group I (b) Operating Fund—Accounts for Designated Items

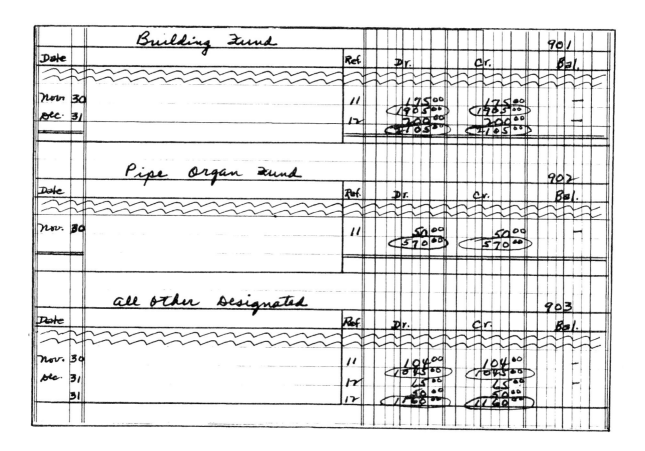

49

The reader is reminded that the budget accounts and accounts for designated items, Groups I(*a*) and (*b*) respectively, are established for each budget period of one year. Thus, each year the bookkeeping process begins with a new set of accounts with zero balances.

Posting to Ledger

While the order of posting from the journal (Exhibit 6-1) is unimportant, it is important that all postings be made or else the ledger will not balance. The order followed here is from left to right for column totals and from top to bottom for the "other" columns. A check mark is placed by each amount in the journal after the posting is made.

Beginning with the cash column, both the debit and credit totals are posted. Columns 3 through 6 are debits and require only a single posting for each. Column 7, kitchen, has a total for debits and a total for credits. Again, it would be possible here to post a single net figure. But to keep a complete record in the kitchen account of both receipts and payments, both amounts are posted. Column 8 is used for recording salaries for the pastor and secretary, accounts 501 and 503, and the total for each account is posted. Account 610, represented by two columns, numbers 9 and 10, is a single ledger account. It is the budget account for F.I.C.A. payroll tax expense. The account is also used to record payroll taxes withheld and their subsequent payment. It serves as a clearing account for this purpose, but at the end of the year the accumulated debit should be only the church's matching portion of F.I.C.A. taxes. (As mentioned earlier, in an effort to keep transactions within the same month, any payroll taxes withheld even if they are not due to be deposited until the month following should be entered as a disbursement in the current month. There is usually some delay in making the actual deposit since it is not due until the fifteenth of the month following. State income taxes withheld, if paid only once each quarter, will not be cleared out until the final month of the quarter. In our illustration the payment of state income taxes withheld of $126 as of December 31 represents withholdings for October, November, and December. Federal taxes for October and November—F.I.C.A. and income taxes withheld, including the F.I.C.A. matching portion—were deposited by the fifteenth of November and December respectively. December's taxes will be deposited by the end of January.)

Budget receipts, column 11, are posted as a credit to account 201. Several postings must be made for "other accounts" in columns 12 and 13. Before any postings are made, accounts that have more than one amount should be recapped, or combined, as is done for account 607 for car allowance. As a result, only one posting to the ledger would be needed for each account. The total posted to car allowance, $211, is the sum of three debits ($100 + $100 + $11 = $211). A special word of explanation is needed for

account 903, designated amounts—other. Since it is necessary that appropriate disposition be made of each designated gift, a separate posting should be made to the account for each such gift. Subsequently, when the payment is made of the gift, the account will contain a record showing the detail of the receipt and its disposition. The reader should observe that each amount in the "other" columns, columns 12 and 13, has been posted individually or else recapped, as was done for the car allowances.

Computing Account Balances

After completing all postings and double checking to determine that every posted amount has a check mark beside it, the next step in the bookkeeping process is to compute the account balances and take a trial balance. Only by taking a trial balance are you certain that amounts have been posted and accumulated accurately. Beginning with the cash account, to the November 30 balance of $568 is added December receipts, $7,478, and deducted December disbursements, $4,289. The balance at December 31, $3,757, is entered in pencil. As a rule, it is easier to distinguish between debit and credit balances by using a black pencil for debit balances and either parentheses or a red pencil for credit balances. The trial balance may be simply added by machine without preparing a list of the accounts, but many bookkeepers prefer to make a list so that the items may be checked more easily. (See exhibit 6-3).

The sample trial balance actually balances! Does this mean that no errors were made? Not necessarily. It is possible that errors could be made in several ways that would not be disclosed by the trial balance. For example, if an amount is posted to the wrong account, it would not become known until someone looked at the charges in that account and found the incorrect charges. Where the amounts involved are fairly large, the error could be discovered when comparing actual amounts with the budget.

Bank Reconciliation

Before preparing financial statements, one should complete the bank reconciliation. The reconciliation is necessary not only to determine possible bank errors but also to detect possible errors in recording bank deposits and checks. Steps in the reconciliation are as follows:

1. Sort checks in numerical order.

2. Beginning with the list of checks outstanding at the end of the previous month, usually in the form of an adding machine tape, compare each returned check to the list to determine which checks have cleared and which are still outstanding. After checking off all the returned checks from the previous outstanding list, continue the procedure for checks recorded in the disbursements journal in the current month. Place a check mark beside each check returned so that a list of the now outstanding checks can be readily

EXHIBIT 6-3
SAMPLE CHURCH TRIAL BALANCE
Twelve months ended, December 31, 1979

	Dr.	Cr.
Cash in checking	3,757	
Operating fund balance (Jan. 1)		1,401
Cash in savings	20,350	
	12,427	
Pipe organ fund balance— restricted		6,025
Fund balance in savings— unrestricted		1,898
Budget receipts		61,116
Denominational missions	9,167	
Local missions	394	
Other missions	310	
Literature & training materials	1,595	
Women's mission & auxiliaries	600	
Brotherhood & auxiliaries	580	
Music & choirs	1,216	
College & youth	750	
Library	204	
Pastor	15,000	
Minister of youth & music	600	
Church secretary	7,200	
Janitorial	1,350	
Part-time help	180	
Office supplies & bulletins	1,905	
Postage	820	
Utilities	3,511	
Telephone	656	
Property insurance	645	
Kitchen	857	
Car allowance & mileage	2,589	
Conventions & conferences	480	
Hospital insurance & retirement	1,439	
F.I.C.A. tax expense	354	
Publicity, advertising, & promotion	352	
Flowers, decorations	296	
Other—contingency	730	
Maintenance—building & grounds	905	
Maintenance—office & other	1,282	
Equipment purchases	1,193	
Debt retirement	1,600	
Building fund	—	
Pipe organ fund	—	
All other designated	—	
	$82,867	$82,867

prepared—by observing those not checked off.

3. From the list for the previous month's checks outstanding not cleared as well as those from the current month's disbursements, prepare a list of checks outstanding.

4. Compare bank deposits recorded on the books with the deposits on the bank statement, and determine if any deposits are not recorded on the bank statement.

5. Determine if any items appear on the bank statement representing checks returned for insufficient funds, service charges for printing checks, etc., and enter them on the reconciliation.

The information gathered above along with other pertinent data is then entered on a reconciliation form similar to the following:

Sample Church, Bank Reconciliation, December 31, 1979

Balance per bank statement, Dec. 31	$5,422
Add: Deposits in transit	—
Less: Outstanding checks (see list)	1,665
Other: Bank charges, errors, etc.	—
Balance, per books, Dec. 31	$3,757

List of Outstanding Checks at Dec. 31, 1979	
# 97 (Nov.)	15
118	768
119	126
120	394
121	47
122	65
123	200
124	50
Total	1,665

The list of outstanding checks reveals only one check, #97 for $15, written in November that did not clear the bank in December. If the list of checks outstanding at November 30 were reproduced above as well, it would disclose that all of the remaining November checks were checked off as having cleared. In the December reconciliation above, there were no deposits in transit. Also there were no additional items that entered into the reconciliation. A bank service charge of $4 for December that appeared on the bank statement, and for which a bank debit memo was enclosed, was recorded in the cash receipts and disbursements journal as of December 31 (refer to Exhibit 6-1). If the bookkeeper elects to delay until the following month the recording of bank charges, such items will appear in the current month's bank reconciliation. For example, in the above case, if the $4 item deducted by the bank in December had not already been entered in December disbursements, you would add it back to the bank statement balance to arrive at the book balance. The reader should note that the balance above, $3,757, agrees with the balance in the ledger account for cash (101) at December 31.

For most bookkeepers, the above reconciliation would be all that is necessary. But some bookkeepers go one step further and derive a cash balance per books even before the cash receipts and disbursements journal is posted to the ledger. For example, for Sample Church, the following information would be taken from the cash receipts and disbursements column totals after all checks and deposits had been entered and the journal balanced:

Cash in bank, Nov. 30 (per ledger)	$ 568
Add: Deposits per books	7,478
Less: Disbursements per books	4,289
Other items: errors in recording checks, etc.	—
Cash balance, per books, Dec. 31	$3,757

The above computation enables the bookkeeper to make a rather quick check on clerical accuracy before ledger postings are made in ink. In fact it is usually somewhat comforting to know the bank account and books reconcile before proceeding to make any of the postings to the ledger. That both checks and deposits were either found in agreement originally or else were subsequently corrected after the reconciliation gives reasonable assurance the trial balance and statements will be in balance.

Information needed to prepare the financial reports has been developed at this point. All that is needed is to extract from the trial balance and ledger accounts the desired data. This step is presented in the next and final chapter on preparation of reports.

Closing the Books

One bookkeeping step remains, that of closing the books. In our example this is done by simply computing the excess of receipts over disbursements (or deficiency if disbursements exceed receipts) within the Group 1 (*a*) and (*b*) accounts and entering this amount in the operating fund balance account (#111). Since the amount of the excess or deficiency is computed when the report is prepared (illustrated in the next chapter), you should make the closing entry after preparation of the report. The information needed to close the books for Sample Church is contained in Exhibit 7-2.

In Part A of Exhibit 7-2, the column on the right contains information for the year ended December 31, 1979. The excess of receipts over disbursements is computed as follows:

Total receipts	$64,951
Less total disbursements	62,595
Excess of receipts over disbursements	$ 2,356

When the $2,356 excess is posted as a credit to account 111 (see Exhibit 6-2), the fund balance then becomes $3,757 ($1,401 + 2,356 = $3,757) and equals the cash in checking (account 101), also $3,757.

At this point two procedures are possible for the actual

closing of Group I(*a*) and (*b*) accounts. The first is to remove the pages for these accounts from the ledger and insert new pages, properly headed, for the transactions of the next year. The second is to rule the accounts at the bottom and thereby separate the transactions for next year (See Accounts 201 through 903 on sample ledger pages, Exhibit 6-2.) from the current year. The ruling, in effect, closes the account, making the balance zero. The latter procedure is illustrated here. By retaining the same accounts in this fashion, it is more convenient to obtain information pertaining to the past year or years. Of course, when both sides of the ledger page have been filled, the old page should be removed and a new page inserted. The old ledger accounts should be filed in proper sequence for future reference. The reader should also observe that we did not close the other ledger accounts—the cash in checking, cash in savings, and respective fund balance accounts. These accounts are used to keep a running balance and are carried forward indefinitely.

Cash Disbursements Records for Building Programs and/or Special Projects

Occasionally, the need arises to open a second checking account. For example, if your church enters into a building program that involves making numerous payments to contractors and subcontractors, it is usually best to keep these transactions out of the operating account. Of course, if only a few payments are to be made to a general contractor, these can be made from the operating account. However, when this is done, it will be necessary to report them separately to distinguish them from normal budget items.

Chapter 7
Reporting

The purpose of reporting is to keep each church member informed about financial matters. An informed member is better able to help the church in fulfilling its mission. A question frequently asked is, "How much information should be reported and how often are reports needed?" In practice, both the frequency of reporting and the amount of detail to be provided vary considerably among churches. Assuming that a detailed budget is approved by the membership at the beginning of the year, it follows that a report of actual results should be made available periodically, comparing this report with the budget. While each church must decide on its reporting needs, the report forms illustrated in this chapter should be adequate for most churches.

The discussion that follows includes reports that present two basic types of information to the member:

1. Reports on receipts and disbursements
2. Reports on fund balances

Also included is a brief reminder about the requirements for filing payroll tax returns and the payment of taxes. Finally, the church should mail to each member a copy of the giver's record.

One method of reporting not considered here is simply to prepare a report that lists the checks written for the period. While this kind of report would give the payee and amount, it would not show the expenditures properly classified by budget accounts. Also, it would not show the cumulative results for the months prior. It is therefore considered inadequate for most churches.

Receipts and Disbursements

Our illustrations are limited to a reporting format that presents actual results along with the budget. It is also possible but less informative to report only the actual results and omit the budget data. In earlier chapters we illustrated how to account for receipts that were designated or restricted as well as those that were undesignated. Likewise, disbursements were illustrated for both of these categories. Since receipts and disbursements of undesignated amounts are identified with the general budget, reporting for these items should be kept separate from designated gifts. Earlier examples included funds in two separate accounts: a checking account through which all receipts and disbursements are channeled and a savings account in which both designated and undesignated funds are kept to earn interest. Thus, our reports must show the following:

1. Activity or flow of cash in the checking account to include:
   Undesignated receipts and budgeted disbursements
   Designated (restricted) receipts and disbursements
2. Activity in the savings account involving designated funds as well as any that are undesignated
3. In addition to reporting the activity in each fund, reports must also show cash balances available.

In our examples of budget expenditures, reports are presented in considerable detail showing all accounts. Some churches may find this much detail to be unnecessary. Also, the examples present information for the current month as well as for the year to date. It would be possible to present the current month only and omit the year-to-date figures. Also, while not considered as desirable, it would be possible to report only the year-to-date information and omit the current month. Fund balances can be included, showing the balance at the beginning of the month only, or be expanded to show both current and beginning of year balances. Special reports may be necessary when a complete summary is needed of the organ fund, building fund, or other such funds that extend over a period of one or more years. For example, the sale of church bonds to finance a new building would require at some point a complete accounting of all activity from date of inception to completion of the project. Reports of this type, while no specific illustration is given here, would be similar to reports prepared in this chapter showing the activity in the fund and the balance at the end.

The first report illustrated is for undesignated receipts and budgeted disbursements and contains Parts A and B (see Exhibit 7-1). This report is of particular interest to organizational leaders and committees responsible for spending budgeted funds. The report is a continuation of the information for Sample Church. It was prepared from the trial balance (Exhibit 6-3). Also, as explained below, data for the current month's receipts and disbursements was taken directly from the accounts in the ledger.

In Part A of the report the first column shows undesignated actual receipts and disbursements for the current month. For the month of December, Sample Church had budgeted receipts of $6,678 and expenditures of $3,489, an excess of budget receipts over expenditures of $3,189. Information for the year to date is reported in the middle column. For Sample Church, the fiscal year ends on December 31. Therefore, this column is for the twelve-month period ending December 31. You will observe on the bottom line that budget receipts exceeded expenditures by $2,356 for the year. This excess of receipts over expenditures means that the cash position is somewhat improved at the end of the year over the beginning.

The reader should note that the amounts for receipts and payments for the month of December in the first column do not appear as such in the trial balance (Exhibit 6-3). The trial balance amounts shown are accumulations and results of activities for the twelve-month period. The amounts for December are included in the balances. But to derive the December figures, it is necessary to refer to the individual general ledger accounts.

The ledger accounts, from which the trial balance was prepared, are shown in chapter 6. To obtain the information for December from account 201 (Budget Receipts), you must select from the account the amounts posted for December, in this case a total of $6,678. To complete the December column, this process is simply repeated by listing the appropriate amounts from each of the undesignated accounts. It is possible that some accounts will have several postings for a given month. When this occurs, the amounts are combined into a single figure for the report. Further discussion is offered below for accounts that contain both receipts and payments.

The final column is the budget information for the same time period as the year-to-date actual amounts reported in the middle column. In preparing the budget column for the first month, and for each month thereafter, it would be necessary to convert the annual budget amount to the fractional time period involved. For example, in the report prepared for the previous month, the budget amount for each item would be 11/12 of the annual amount. Also, the report prepared for the first month of each fiscal period would be unlike that of any other month. It would contain only two columns instead of three. The first column would report the actual results for that month, which would also be the year-to-date information, and the second column would present the budget for one month.

Report Analysis

In the example, we can see that actual receipts for the twelve months exceeded the $60,000 budget amount by approximately $1,100—to be exact $1,116. On the next to the bottom line, notice that total disbursements of $58,760 are less than the $60,000 amount in the budget column. By spending approximately $1,200 less than the approved budget, the year-end cash position was thereby improved. While the total picture has been briefly observed, no attention has been given to individual budget accounts. Most readers would require a few minutes to scan the report line by line observing the actual versus budget amounts. When the report is presented before the church at the business session, it should be given in summary only. By giving totals for the major categories and answering questions, the report can be made within a brief time period. In no case should the entire report be read to the members. By distributing copies at the beginning of the business sessions, those who wish to read it over usually have time to do so. In the analysis here, no attempt will be made to describe variations in each account. However, several comments are offered for unusual items.

Disbursements for denominational missions, $9,167 for the year, exceeded the budget of $9,000. In Sample Church, payments for denominational missions are a fixed percentage of budget receipts—15 percent. Since receipts exceeded the budget by $1,116, as referred to above, denominational missions would be approximately $160 in excess of the budget of $9,000 (to be exact, $1,116 x .15 = $167).

In all other budget categories, the budget amount exceeded the actual disbursements. But for some individual items within categories, the actual spent exceeded the budget. For example, $1,216 was spent for music and choirs, and the budget was $1,200. The library account is also slightly over the budget. How much variation should be permissible, if any? And what is the role of the finance committee or treasurer in this regard? As suggested earlier, some flexibility in spending is desirable, or else undue red tape and inconvenience will result. The finance committee should at least be permitted to make adjustments for most items as long as the budget total is not exceeded. The most important exception is the amount budgeted for salaries and allowances. These should be subject to change only by church action. On the other hand, if the utility bills exceed the budget, there is no alternative but to pay them. The finance committee as well as the entire church should keep in mind that the budget can be a useful tool in the allocation of resources. It must not be considered inflexible and be allowed to defeat worthwhile objectives and programs. Of course, the proper time for exercising control and fiscal restraint is not after the fact but beforehand when expenditure requests are made.

One other account deserves a brief comment. The kitchen account reflects the net of receipts and expenditures. For the month of December, receipts exceeded expenditures by $295, and the net amount is shown in parentheses. The net

EXHIBIT 7-1
SCHEDULE I
Part A

Reporting

SAMPLE CHURCH
STATEMENT OF CASH RECEIPTS AND DISBURSEMENTS
for the month ended December 31 and for the twelve-month period ended December 31, 1979

UNDESIGNATED	Actual		Budget for twelve months ended Dec. 31, 1979
	Month of December	Twelve months ended Dec. 31, 1979	
BUDGET RECEIPTS	$6,678	$61,116	$60,000
BUDGET DISBURSEMENTS:			
Missions			
Denominational	1,002	9,167	9,000
Local	—	394	400
Other	—	310	300
Total	1,002	9,871	9,700
Educational Ministry			
Literature, materials & supplies	54	1,595	1,600
Women's mission & auxiliaries	—	600	600
Brotherhood & auxiliaries	—	580	600
Music & choirs	29	1,216	1,200
College & youth	—	750	800
Library	6	204	200
Total	89	4,945	5,000
Personnel Salaries & Allowances			
Pastor	1,250	15,000	15,000
Minister of youth & music	—	600	1,200
Church secretary	600	7,200	7,200
Janitorial	—	1,350	1,400
Part-time help	—	180	200
Total	1,850	24,330	25,000
General Operations			
Office supplies & bulletins	4	1,905	1,900
Postage	65	820	850
Utilities	133	3,511	3,600
Telephone	68	656	720
Property insurance	—	645	650
Kitchen	(295)	857	900
Car allowance & mileage	211	2,589	2,600
Conventions & conferences	—	480	500
Hospital insurance & retirement	47	1,439	1,452
F.I.C.A. tax expense	120	354	432
Publicity, advertising, & promotion	—	352	360
Flowers, decorations	18	296	300
Other—contingency	—	730	936
Total	371	14,634	15,200
Property & Equipment			
Maintenance—building & grounds	28	905	1,000
Maintenance—office & other	22	1,282	1,300
Equipment purchases	—	1,193	1,200
Total	50	3,380	3,500
Debt retirement	127	1,600	1,600
Total disbursements	3,489	58,760	60,000
Excess (or deficiency) of receipts over disbursements	$3,189	$ 2,356	$

Part B

DESIGNATED	Month of December		12 months ended Dec. 31	
	Receipts	Payments	Receipts	Payments
Building fund*	$200	$200	$2,105	$2,105
Pipe organ fund*	—	—	570	570
All other	115	115	1,160	1,160
Total	$315	$315	$3,835	$3,835

*These payments are transfers to the savings account: for December, $200; for the year, $2,675.

amount for year to date, $857, is below the budget of $900. It would be possible as an alternative reporting procedure to insert both receipts and payments on the same line, as follows:

Kitchen (receipts, $170; payments $465), $295

By the addition of another line, it would be possible to give the same information for the year-to-date column. A similar approach could be followed for any account that involves both receipts and payments.

Part B is a continuation of Schedule I. It is a report of designated receipts and payments also showing the current month and the year to date. For Sample Church, the month is December and the twelve-month period is for the year ended December 31, 1979. In keeping with the nature of designated items, Part B has columns for receipts as well as payments with no budget information being shown. While the church may not wish to promote the making of gifts for designated causes, nevertheless, members who make such gifts wish to see that they are properly reported and accounted for.

These funds flow through the checking account just as do the undesignated funds. As soon as the funds are received, they are usually paid out, preferably within the same month. In our example, Sample Church has received and paid out the same amounts for the month of December and also for the twelve-month period, totals of $315 and $3,835 respectively. An asterisk (*) is used to denote payments that are simply transfers to another fund—in this example to the savings account, shown in Schedule II, Part B. The amount of detail to be reported for designated gifts will vary considerably from church to church. Most churches would report separately amounts received from fund drives to promote purchases of buildings and equipment. In addition, when special appeals are made for such causes as local and foreign missions, these gifts should be reported separately. Organizational leaders who promote such offerings, as well as the members at large, desire to know progress made toward reaching the goals. As a rule, the report to the membership should give enough information, without giving unnecessary detail, to keep the members apprised as to progress. Use of an "other" category for summarizing small amounts will help.

Fund Balances

Reports showing cash balances in various church funds are fairly simple when compared with the previous report on budget expenditures. Only a few lines are needed, making the results easier to comprehend. For Sample Church, fund balances are reported in Schedule II, Parts A and B.

Part A is shown first, with Part B immediately following. (See exhibit 7-2.)

Part A of the report shows the beginning fund balance, receipts for the month for both undesignated and designated

amounts, and transfers from savings, if any. Next are listed disbursements for these same items. In the first column, December is reported, and in the second column information for the year to date. In the first column the ending cash balance of $3,757 was obtained by adding $6,993 to the beginning balance of $568 and subtracting disbursements of $3,804. The reader should observe that the amounts for receipts and disbursements are taken from totals reported in Schedule I above. In the second column, similar information is shown for the twelve-month period ended December 31. These totals are also taken from Schedule I. The final balance of $3,757 is the same in both columns and is the cash in checking account on December 31, 1979.

The reporting format for Part A is fairly flexible and should permit a church to report almost any kind of receipt or disbursement. For example, if a transfer is made from the savings account to the checking account, the preparer would simply enter it under the caption for receipts—none in our example. Transfers of designated receipts from checking to savings are shown in the example under the disbursements captions, a total of $200 for December and $2,675 for the year. An example of another kind of transfer would occur if next year Sample Church decided to place in savings some of the excess cash in checking. The report for January would list this under disbursements as a fund transfer. Also, a note should be added to explain the nature of the transfer. The amount of the transfer would also be listed in Part B, explained below. Sample Church did not have a transfer of funds from the savings account to checking. Assuming a $500 transfer from the savings account, two separate entries would be necessary, one for each fund involved, as follows:

1. Credit: Account 151		Cash in Savings	500
Debit: Account 170		Fund Balance in Savings—	
		unrestricted	500
(To record the transfer in the savings fund accounts.)			
2. Credit: Account 111		Operating fund balance	500
Debit: Account 101		Cash in checking	500
(To record the transfer in the operating fund accounts.)			

Part B contains information for the savings account for the month of December and for the twelve months ended December 31. A different arrangement is necessary because the amount of cash held for Sample Church is made up of three separate funds—building, pipe organ, and an unrestricted sum. While it would be possible to establish three separate savings accounts—a desirable procedure if the amounts exceed the level of protection afforded by federal deposit insurance—the reporting would be the same. In the first section, transactions for the month of December reflect as receipts a transfer from checking and interest earned. The amounts are $200 and $841 respectively. The beginning balance is $19,309 and the ending balance $20,350.

EXHIBIT 7-2
SCHEDULE II
Part A

SAMPLE CHURCH
SUMMARY OF OPERATING FUND RECEIPTS AND
DISBURSEMENTS AND FUND BALANCES
for the month of December and twelve months
ended December 31, 1979

	Month of December	Twelve-month period Jan. 1 through Dec. 31, 1979	Supporting Schedule
Beginning balance	$ 568	$ 1,401	
Add: Undesignated receipts	6,678	61,116	Schedule I, Part A
Designated receipts	315	3,835	Schedule I, Part B
Transfers from savings	—	—	
Total	$6,993	$64,951	
Less: Budgeted disbursements	3,489	58,760	Schedule I, Part A
Designated disbursements	115	1,160	Schedule I, Part B
Transfers to savings	200	2,675	Schedule I, Part B
Total	$3,804	$62,595	
Balance, December 31	$3,757	$ 3,757	

Part B

Summary of Savings Account Receipts and
Disbursements and Fund Balances
for month of December, 1979

		Receipts			
	Balance Nov. 30, 1979	Transfers from checking	Interest earned	Disbursements	Balance Dec. 31, 1979
Building fund	$11,747	$200	$480		$12,427
Pipe organ fund	5,771		254		6,025
Unrestricted	1,791		107		1,898
Total	$19,309	$200	$841		$20,350

For year ended December 31, 1979

		Receipts			
	Balance Jan. 1, 1979	Transfers from checking	Interest earned	Disbursements	Balance Dec. 31, 1979
Building fund	$ 9,842	$2,105	$480		$12,427
Pipe organ fund	5,201	570	254		6,025
Unrestricted	1,791		107		1,898
Total	$16,834	$2,675	$841		$20,350

The lower portion of Part B is a summary of activity for the year ended December 31, 1979. Both portions of this part are arranged in the same manner. While it is possible to report the interest at the time it is credited to the savings account by the bank, usually quarterly, in our example the amount is reported only once for the entire year. For Sample Church, the amount, $841, was obtained by adding the interest credited to the savings passbook for each quarter. The amount was divided among the funds by obtaining an approximate average of the fund balances in each account for the year.

The reader should observe that in Part A of Schedule II is reported the total stewardship effort for Sample Church. Giving for the year for all causes was $64,951. The amount for designated causes, $3,835, was deposited in the checking account and also disbursed from the checking account. Of this amount $2,675 was transferred to savings, leaving designated disbursements of $1,160. Therefore, to obtain the total of disbursements for budget and designated causes, excluding transfers, it is necessary to add two amounts together. For Sample Church, the total spent for all causes, excluding transfers, was $59,920 ($58,760 + 1,160 = $59,920).

Alternative Reporting Format

There are a number of possible formats for presenting financial information. An alternative form of reporting is presented in Exhibit 7-3 that gives considerably less detail than the one above but achieves the same overall results. As stated earlier, the financial report to the church membership should include (1) information on receipts and disbursements and (2) fund balances.

Exhibit 7-3 presents both the checking account and savings account transactions as well as their balances. Observe first that the checking account portion includes both undesignated and designated receipts and disbursements. The amounts were taken from Parts A and B of Exhibit 7-1 and Part A of Exhibit 7-2. The information for the savings account was taken from Part B of Schedule II. The question arises as to how the data for budget categories would be summarized for Exhibit 7-3 when the preparer does not have available Exhibit 7-2. In that case, it would be necessary for the preparer first to list the accounts and obtain totals for each category. These totals would then be entered on the report.

By reviewing the columnar arrangement, you will see that it is the same as Exhibit 7-1—including a column for December, for twelve months ended December 31, and the budget for the twelve-month period. While budget receipts are the same in both exhibits, only the total disbursements by major categories are presented in Exhibit 7-3. If more detail is needed for some of the accounts with larger balances—such as for utilities that total $3,511 for the year

(Exhibit 7-1) and literature $1,595—they could be listed separately.

As in the earlier example for Sample Church, there is an excess of receipts over disbursements for December and for the twelve-month period—$3,189 and $2,356 respectively. In this report, these amounts will be combined with the results of the undesignated transactions presented next. When disbursements exceed receipts, a deficiency, it would be necessary to indicate this deficiency by showing the amounts in parentheses.

In the designated section of the report, receipts are listed first using the same breakdown as in Exhibit 7-1, showing both December and year-to-date totals. When the disbursements were deducted, most of which were transfers to the savings account, there were no balances remaining—all receipts were disposed of in the same period. However, this condition does not always exist. In such cases, there may be either an excess of receipts over payments or an excess of payments over receipts—a deficiency. Finally, the excess of receipts over disbursements, for both designated and undesignated, when added to the beginning balance in checking, gives the ending balance in the account, $3,757 in both columns—the sum of (1) $3,189, (2) 0, and (4) $568, equals $3,757. A line has also been included for other transfers to or from the savings account—none in our example. If the church wishes to keep any excess cash invested and earning interest, it may be necessary to make frequent transfers between checking and savings accounts. Thus, by using the above described format, it is possible to show all the information pertaining to the checking account within the same exhibit. The savings account data, presented in the bottom portion of Exhibit 7-3, is arranged in a different manner than was done in Exhibit 7-2. Also, the transactions for the month of December are not shown separately. Here they are combined with the twelve-month data. You will observe that each fund is shown in a separate column—building fund, pipe organ fund, and unrestricted balance—with a separate column for totals. In Exhibit 7-2, the funds were listed horizontally with the transactions shown in vertical columns.

On the first line, fund balances at January 1 of the current year are presented, a total of $16,834. Next are the current year's additions, a total of $3,516, consisting of transfers from checking account, $2,675, and interest earned, $841. Since the amounts transferred from the checking account have already been identified in the report—building fund, $2,105, and pipe organ fund, $570—only the total is shown here. Finally, interest earned, $841, is an addition to the savings account and to the respective funds. This amount, of course, does not appear on the report for the checking account since it did not flow through that account. Disbursements and any other fund transfers—none in our example —would be listed next. If your church would like

EXHIBIT 7-3

CHECKING ACCOUNT—STATEMENT OF CASH RECEIPTS,
DISBURSEMENTS, AND FUND BALANCES
for the month ended December 31 and
for the twelve-month period ended December 31, 1979

| | | Actual | | Budget for |
| | | Month of December | Twelve months ended Dec. 31, 1979 | twelve months ended Dec. 31, 1979 |
UNDESIGNATED				
BUDGET RECEIPTS		$6,687	$61,116	$60,000
BUDGET DISBURSEMENTS:				
Missions		1,002	9,871	9,700
Educational Ministry		89	4,945	5,000
Personnel Salaries and Allowances		1,850	24,330	25,000
General Operations		371	14,634	15,200
Property and Equipment		50	3,380	3,500
Debt Retirement		127	1,600	1,600
Total Disbursements		3,489	58,760	60,000
Excess of receipts over disbursements—undesignated	(1)	3,189	2,356	-0-
DESIGNATED				
RECEIPTS:				
Building fund		200*	2,105*	
Pipe organ fund		—	570	
All other		115	1,160	
Total		315	3,835	
DISBURSEMENTS:				
Transfers to savings acct.		200*	2,675*	
All other		115	1,160	
Total		315	3,835	
Excess of receipts over disbursements—designated	(2)	-0-	-0-	
Other—transfers to (or from) savings	(3)	-0-	-0-	
Checking account balance at beginning of period	(4)	568	1,401	
Checking account balance at Dec. 31 [sum of (1), (2), (3), and (4)]		$3,757	$3,757	

*These amounts are deposited in the checking account and subsequently transferred to the savings account—see below.

SAVINGS ACCOUNT—STATEMENT OF CASH RECEIPTS,
DISBURSEMENTS, AND FUND BALANCES
for the twelve-month period ended December 31, 1979

	Building Fund	Pipe Organ Fund	Unrestricted Balance	Total
Balance, Jan. 1, 1979	$ 9,842	$5,201	$1,791	$16,834
Add:				
Amounts transferred from checking account	2,105	570		2,675
Interest earned	480	254	107	841
Total	2,585	824	107	3,516
Deduct:				
Disbursements and fund transfers	—	—	—	—
Balance, Dec. 31, 1979	$12,427	$6,025	$1,898	$20,350

for the report to show a separate breakdown of December receipts and payments, it would be necessary to prepare a schedule similar to the Savings Account portion of Exhibit 7-3. Instead of showing the balance at January 1, the first line would show the balance at December 1. Likewise, the receipts and disbursements would be for December alone.

You may use one of the reporting forms presented above, or you may wish to experiment with different arrangements of data within the reports until you discover the one that best suits both you and the church congregation.

Noncash Donations

Members and their families frequently donate significant items of property to the church either in addition to or in lieu of cash contributions. Such donations should be entered on the member's giving record at their cash equivalent value. The nature of the property and the fair value should in turn be reported in a note appended to the financial report, preferably at the bottom of Schedule I, or else on a separate sheet attached.

Payroll Tax Filing and Reporting

The financial secretary or treasurer should determine the requirements for withholding and filing federal and state payroll tax.

Federal income taxes. The church is required to withhold income tax from employees' wages. A tax booklet is provided by the Internal Revenue Service giving the amounts. Only ordained ministers (as defined by tax law) are not taxed on amounts designated as rental or housing allowances and utilities. The minister's wages subject to withholding would be the base salary, excluding housing as well as car allowances. (Please refer to the latest tax booklets for up-to-date requirements.)

As defined in tax laws, ministers are not employees. They may elect to pay their income taxes quarterly on an estimated basis as do self-employed persons. However, the regulations state that by voluntary agreement the church may withhold the tax each pay period.

Income taxes withheld are combined with Social Security and Medicare taxes and are deposited on a regular basis.

Social Security and Medicare taxes (formerly F.I.C.A. taxes). All church employees except ministers are subject to Social Security and Medicare taxes. The church is required to match the amount withheld from the employee. Rates (1996) are as follows: Social Security—6.2 percent on the first $62,700 in wages; Medicare—1.45 percent on all wages paid.

As self-employed persons, ministers are responsible for paying their own Social Security and self-employment tax at the self-employed rate. Ministers must include the rental value of the home and related allowances as earnings from self-employment for purposes of the Social Security

self-employment tax. (Note: Ministers have the option of choosing not to participate in the Social Security system, but once the choice has been made, it is irrevocable.)

Federal rules state that employers should deposit withheld income, Social Security, and Medicare taxes with the employer's matching portion in an authorized financial institution. The amount of taxes determines the frequency of deposits; most churches will be required to make at least monthly deposits (refer to *Employer's Tax Guide*).

Each quarter, the church is required to file a return (Form 941) showing the amount of wages and the related taxes. In addition, within a specified period, the church must provide each employee with a statement of wages paid and taxes withheld (Form W-2).

Advance payment of earned income credit. Regulations (in 1996) state that if you are an employee, your employer can pay you an advance earned income credit up to $1,291. To claim the credit, both the employee's earned income and adjusted gross income must be less than $25,078. At the same time an employee files his or her federal income tax return, other supplemental credits may apply depending on the number of qualifying children; however, the maximum basic credit is $1,291 with one qualifying child.

To summarize briefly (refer to *Employer's Tax Guide* for further rules and exceptions), employees eligible for the earned income credit (EIC) may either receive it on their personal tax returns or in advance payments during the year. Employees who want it in advance must file Form W-5 with you, their employer. As employer, you are required to notify employees not having income tax withheld that they may be eligible for a tax refund because of the EIC.

Figure the advance EIC payment and include it with wages paid to eligible employees who have filed Form W-5. Enter the amount of advance EIC payments on your employment tax return as a deduction from the combined payroll withholdings.

Federal and state unemployment taxes. Churches are exempt from these taxes.

State income taxes. Most states that have an income tax require the employer to withhold the tax each pay period. The requirements for withholding and subsequent payment are similar to those for federal income taxes. The church should request a copy of the latest tax booklet and any instructions that may be necessary.

Mailing Givers' Records

Mailing copies of records to givers checks the accuracy of the church's record keeping and also informs members of amounts given to date. The form used for givers' records should provide sufficient copies for quarterly mailings, including the final mailing at the end of the year, which is important for tax records.

Chapter 8
Computer Applications

Computers now process a wide variety of the financial as well as nonfinancial data found in churches of all sizes. As church treasurer, perhaps you would like to know how to make your bookkeeping task easier. In larger churches, the greatest need may be that of keeping church membership records. In our discussion of computer capabilities, we will first consider broad applications that include the total church function and then accounting and financial applications to help you with the extended illustrations of bookkeeping for Sample Church.

Getting Acquainted with Computers and Computer Software

Computers come in many different shapes and sizes. Small personal computers are now available with capabilities that far exceed the large mainframe computers first used in business and government. Mass production and a highly competitive market have made personal computers affordable for churches as well as homes. Costing under three thousand dollars, a complete computer installation consists of a processor (the brains), a keyboard for entering instructions and data, a monitor (or screen) for viewing data being processed, and a printer. These hardware items will perform only according to your instructions (programs or software) that tell the processor what to do. As you may have suspected already, the key to success is to have the right programs. Again, a highly competitive software market has made available a variety of good programs. While the cost of some of the more specialized programs exceeds the cost of the hardware itself, generalized accounting packages (written for small-business applications) can be purchased for under several hundred dollars. Information on program content and availability is presented in a later paragraph. Detailed instructions are usually provided with the software to help you install it and tell you how to use it.

While shopping for hardware, keep in mind the size and type of computer needed to run the software you intend to purchase. Software providers are careful to specify this information. Most of the machines with hard disks have more than enough capacity to store programs and data for even the largest churches. You will want to make sure the computer you purchase is one with a hard disk.

Where to Buy a Computer

Buyers have a wide choice among different manufacturers and models. A local computer store or dealer is a good place to start. After looking at dealer showrooms, reading literature, seeing demonstrations, and gaining some hands-on experience, you will be better able to talk the language and make the right decision. Consider also the possibility of mail order as well as used machines available from users who have outgrown their current models. While computers require little upkeep, be sure you understand how to get service when the need arises.

Computer Software in General

As mentioned earlier, you must have a program (software), or set of instructions, that tells the computer exactly how to process, file, and print your church's data. Software providers have been busy in the past ten years or so writing a variety of programs to fit almost any need. Many of the systems packages can be purchased in one or more modules, thus allowing you to install either a total system or part of a system. Wherever possible, try to anticipate church growth and changing software needs. In our discussion, church software packages are classified as either administrative or accounting. The following software modules serve church administration functions:

A. *Administration—Membership.* Some programs break membership into several modules. One module keeps track of names and addresses as well as personal data. Additional modules can be added to track pledges, contributions, attendance, and prospects. Output from these modules includes mailing lists for selected mailings as well as data for printing a church directory.

B. *Administration—Other.* Examples here are programs written for library activity and music, as well as for keeping information on sermons and sermon titles.

Modules in the accounting category cover the complete accounting system. The following list is representative of modules currently available:

A. *General ledger package (usually includes budgeting).* Depending on the software vendor, this program should be adequate to do the complete accounting cycle and print the financial reports. To enable posting of contributions to givers' records, the member-contribution module is also required.

B. *Other accounting modules.* Other modules frequently used in larger applications include accounts payable and check writing, payroll, and property and equipment.

A second possibility for keeping church books is to use one of the accounting programs written for small-business applications. Before specialized church software became available, many accountants in the church field adapted the general ledger packages developed for business and industry. These programs in today's market usually cost considerably less than church packages but lack some of the features peculiar to church accounting. You could possibly justify spending fifty dollars or so even if you only used the program for a short time.

Finally, if computers are your hobby, you may find more innovative ways to meet your church's accounting needs, such as writing your own program.

Where to Buy Software

While researching your computer purchase, ask about sources of computer software. Obtain a fairly broad sampling, since there is a wide variety from which to choose. Ideally, you can find a church treasurer or an accounting or bookkeeping firm that has already made a similar search. The brief listing in the Appendix will give you a few ideas for starters. Most all programs have more information and capability than is necessary for any one user, especially a smaller church.

Recording Transactions for Sample Church

In the earlier discussion of hand-kept records, the accounting process began with establishing a chart of accounts to serve as a device for collecting and classifying financial data. Next, a budget was developed using the same group of accounts. Transactions involving cash receipts and cash payments were then recorded in a special journal and posted to the ledger accounts. Finally, from these accounts and from budget data, a set of financial reports was prepared. With a computer system, the same information and same process must be completed, beginning with the budget. Make a practice run yourself using data from the extended illustration in chapter 6 for Sample Church.

Budget

Enter budget amounts as specified in your software program, using the account number and titles in the chart of accounts. To enable persons to readily compare actual amounts to budget amounts on a month-by-month basis, divide the annual budget into twelve equal parts. Also, if you report cumulative actual results for succeeding months, provide for cumulative budget amounts.

Cash Payments

Each transaction from the check record must be entered via the computer keyboard, giving the date, payee, and check number, as well as the amount(s) and account number(s) to be debited or credited. Postings to the ledger accounts are done automatically by the computer. Software directions tell you what to do to complete this posting and whether or not a printed check register (similar to Exhibit 6-1) is provided. Since the computer does the posting and ensures accuracy of debits and credits, you do not necessarily need to obtain monthly totals of the journal.

Cash Receipts

Weekly deposit reports (Exhibit 3-4) provide information for journalizing cash receipts. Using the format specified, enter each amount and each account number as well as the deposit total. If the computer program does not automatically check equality of debits and credits, do this manually by adding machine or calculator.

Other Transactions

In addition to the above cash transactions that involved third parties outside the church entity, Sample Church made an internal transfer of funds from the checking account to a savings account (see explanation of check No. 123 for $200.00). To reflect this amount in the building fund (as a fund separate from the operating fund), a similar journal entry is made on the computer to debit Cash in Savings (Ac. 151) and credit Building Fund Balance (Ac. 161). Of course, fund accounting procedures necessitate separate ledger accounts for each fund. (Refer to the illustration at the end of chapter 5 for a review of the relationship between accounts for Group I [operating fund accounts] and Group II [savings accounts].)

End-of-Month Procedure

With pen-and-ink systems, some accountants like to prepare a trial balance (Exhibit 6-3) after manually posting and computing account balances. Skip the trial balance routine here and instruct the computer to print the statement of cash receipts and disbursements (Exhibit 7-1). The report showing fund balances (Exhibit 7-2) can be prepared either by the computer, or in some cases done manually, depending on the software. Also obtain a printout of the general ledger as well as other data for which a hard copy is desired. Printouts serve as a backup in case computer files are lost (see below).

Posting Givers' Records

For computer posting, you must have software installed that maintains a file for each member. Unless the posting is done as you enter cash receipts, a separate posting will be necessary later. By using either preprinted or computer-printed forms, you can prepare the quarterly and/or annual statements and address them for mailing.

Backup Records

Throughout the recording and posting of data, keep a proper backup to ensure that essential information will not be lost. Most systems provide for this eventuality. For example, weekly or monthly printouts will enable you to reconstruct data lost due to computer failure or power outages requiring reprocessing of transactions only since the last printout. When instructed by the computer program to transfer information to a backup disk, be sure to do so. Since you often need to refer back to the general ledger accounts for a prior year, it would be easier to find such information if the computer printout gives the same detail as the hand-posted ledger. Finally, keep your computer, computer programs, and data in a safe place to prevent possible damage or tampering.

Appendix
Software Vendors

The four vendors listed below offer software designed exclusively for churches. The modules that were described earlier may either be purchased separately or, in some cases, in groups that cover all the essential functions. Quoted prices may include a charge for consultation and updating. In addition, some provision must be made for installation cost.

1. F1 Software, 208 Ridgefield Drive, Asheville, North Carolina 28806; 1-800-486-1800; Fax 704-665-1999.
2. Omega C. G. Limited, 377 East Butterfield Road, Suite 675, Lombard, Illinios 60148; 708-969-7799.
3. Parsons Technology, One Parsons Drive, Hiawatha, Iowa 52233; 1-800-223-6925; 24-hour Fax line 319-393-1002.
4. Shelby Systems, Inc., 65 Germantown Court, Suite 303, Cordova, Tennessee 38018; 901-757-2372.

Ask your computer or software dealer to help you locate as many additional software vendors as possible.

Smaller churches that do not want wish to purchase specialized software could consider using a typical general ledger package that a small business would use. This program would enable you to record and post transactions and print financial statements. Member contributions would be manually posted. As example of this kind of software is DacEasy Accounting sold by DacEasy, Inc. (17950 Preston Road, Suite 800, Dallas, Texas 75252; 1-800-322-3279). Software of this type is widely available from a variety of suppliers.

Your denominational offices might also offer information on recommended software. Check with denominattional headquarters for referral to the appropriate department.

Glossary of Terms

Account. A device used for accumulating the data from transactions. The form of the account may vary somewhat, but it must provide space for the transaction date, amount, description, reference to journal source, and whether a debit or credit. Collectively, the accounts constitute the ledger.

Accounting Equation. An expression in algebraic form of the equality of assets and equities. In accounting for funds, as is the case in most churches, the equation is stated as follows:

Assets (cash and other liquid resources) = *Fund Balance*

Assets. The resources owned by an entity are its assets. In the examples throughout this book, the assets are cash and savings accounts. Occasionally churches also invest in other liquid assets, such as treasury bills, certificates of deposit, or money market certificates. Also, it is not uncommon for members to donate to the church shares of corporate stock and corporate bonds. These are to be valued at market price at the time of receipt of the gift and recorded in a separate asset account apart from cash.

Budget. A planning document that focuses on programs and plans for one or more years in advance. It contains budget accounts identified with specific programs and purposes and the anticipated amount of expenditures needed for each account.

Cash Basis vs. Accrual Basis of Accounting. The cash basis is a simplified system of accounting that emphasizes keeping up with and reporting on the flow of cash. In most churches, the accounting system is designed to reflect the actual cash received and cash paid out. The accrual basis, used by many business entities, is designed to record the effect of transactions as they occur. A significant number of their transactions are both sales and purchases made on credit terms with a delay in the payment of cash. Only by recording sales when they are made and costs when they are incurred can the business determine its profit.

Debits and Credits. Abbreviated dr. and cr., the terms refer to the left side and right side, respectively, of an account. When identified with the accounting equation, the normal account balance for assets is debit and for fund balance credit. As shown below decreases in fund balance are recorded as debits and increases in fund balance are recorded as credits.

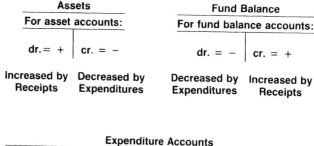

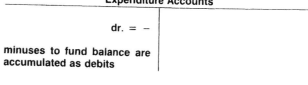

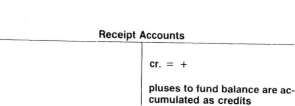

Designated Gifts. Donors occasionally make gifts of money or property and specify the purpose for which it is intended. Also called "restricted gifts," the church should account for and report these separately from the undesignated or unrestricted gifts.

Fiscal Year. Any consecutive twelve-month period adopted by the church for accounting purposes. The calendar year is used most frequently.

Fund Accounting. Churches and other not-for-profit entities usually keep their assets in one or more separate funds. Especially in churches, the emphasis in accounting is to keep up with the inflows and outflows of cash resources and the status of resources in the various funds.

Journal. Called the book of original entry, it is the place where transactions are recorded initially. Transactions are recorded in chronological sequence and analyzed into one or more debit and credit components. Most accounting systems require a general journal (it usually contains two columns for recording amounts) and one or more special journals to expedite the accumulation of data. The examples in this book, however, utilize a single journal that combines the recording of cash receipts and disbursements. Our combined journal also contains two columns so that it serves the same purpose as the general journal making a separate two-column journal unnecessary.

Ledger. See **Account.**

Nondiscretionary vs. Discretionary Expenditures. Certain operating costs such as utilities and payments on mortgage notes are fixed by contract or agreement—nondiscretionary. Other payments or expenditures are largely made at the option of the church—discretionary.

Restricted Gifts. See **Designated Gifts.**

Transaction. An event or activity such as the receipt or payment of cash.

Trial Balance. A list of the ledger accounts and their balances to prove the equality of total debit and credit amounts.

Undesignated Gifts. Gifts of money or property for the general support of the church's program.